RACHEL KHOO'S KITCHEN NOTEBOOK

Rachel Khoo's Kitchen Notebook

over 100 delicious recipes
from my personal cookbook

Photography by David Loftus
Illustrations by Rachel Khoo

CHRONICLE BOOKS
SAN FRANCISCO

First published in the United States of America
in 2015 by Chronicle Books LLC.

Originally published in the United Kingdom in 2015
by Michael Joseph, an imprint of Penguin Books Ltd.

Text copyright © 2015 by Rachel Khoo.

Photographs copyright © 2015 by David Loftus.

Illustrations copyright © 2015 by Peas in a Pot Ltd.

Library of Congress Cataloging-in-Publication Data available.

ISBN 978-1-4521-4056-8

Manufactured in China

10 9 8 7 6 5 4 3 2 1

Chronicle Books LLC
680 Second Street
San Francisco, California 94107
www.chroniclebooks.com

Contents

Introduction

I carry a notebook everywhere and it almost always ends up tattered, dog-eared, and splashed with various food stains from eating my way around the world or cooking in my kitchen. The recipes, illustrations, kitchen tidbits, and tips that end up in my notebook are all something that I wanted to share. The recipes reflect both my culinary past and present, the places I've been, my kitchen experiences . . . making a book that tells the story of how I cook in the kitchen.

After writing two cookbooks that chronicled my exploration of *la cuisine française*, I felt it was time to show my true colors with this book. My childhood played a big part in forming my culinary DNA, but the experiences and cultures I've been exposed to in my adult life have also been formative in the way my cooking style has evolved. The last several years have been packed tighter than a tin of sardines with adventures close to home and beyond. I've visited an eclectic range of places, from the Scandi-cool Stockholm and the fragrant delights of the East in Istanbul to the slightly rough-around-the-edges Naples, and rediscovered my hometown, London, with its vibrant, energetic food scene.

Even though I've lived in Paris for eight years, I am not "that French woman off the telly," as I've frequently been described since the *Little Paris Kitchen* TV show aired. I'm quite proudly British (despite the many years of British food bashing I endured in France), with a colorful culinary heritage, thanks to my Malaysian dad and Austrian mum. Living in Bavaria as a teenager also played its part. My taste buds were stimulated from a young age with spices, flavors, and smells from Southeast Asia, sweet and heartwarming dishes from Austria, as well as some British classics such as roast beef and Yorkshire pudding. Although I had a diverse culinary upbringing, my parents were not snobby when it came to food. They understood the importance of nutritious home-cooked fare and the ritual of sitting down for a meal every day as a family, but the odd fast-food treat or TV dinner was still allowed. My mum has always been a savvy shopper, never wasting a thing and ever-inventive with leftovers. Our so-called "leftovers night," a common thing at home, would often look like the foodie equivalent of a United Colors of Benetton commercial, with schnitzel, shepherd's pie, rendang curry, and stir-fried rice all on the table at the same time. When I look back, I think my parents were unintended foodie visionaries with their leftover fusion food. Eating Austrian dumpling soup with some char siu roasted pork and pickled chiles was not unusual in the Khoo household, and this was back in the '80s, long before Korean tacos or kebab pizza were the norm.

I come from a creative background. I spent four years at art college, working on projects where the main objective was to communicate an idea through a particular medium,

in my case graphic/web design and photography. I was initially drawn to food because it's a way of expressing my creativity with an added tasty bonus. Since I started writing cookbooks, I feel like I have hit the jackpot. It combines many of my passions: creativity, socializing, and eating!

The way I go about creating a recipe book is similar to the creative practice I learned at art college. Just like an art project, it all starts with hands-on research, initial ideas scribbled in my notebook, that evolve into experiments, and then the final piece. I like to travel, to meet people, and to experience the food, culture, flavors, sights, sounds, and smells firsthand, gathering the inspiration and research to feed my brain and tummy with ideas. Those ideas end up being an initial scribble and sketch in my notebook. Then, when it comes to taking the sketch from concept to recipe creation, chaos ensues in the kitchen, with pots, pans, and many ingredients being thrown around. More often than not, the recipe does not turn out quite the way I imagined on paper. However, even the failures are usually successes: I might discover a new flavor combination, or texture, or cooking technique. If it's really a total disaster, it ultimately helps me to write a better recipe, as I'll then understand what can go wrong in the kitchen. I always believe that failures are part of the process. It's how you deal with them that will eventually influence whether you succeed or not.

Famous communication philosopher Marshall McLuhan once said that "the medium is the message." A cookbook has a tactile and personal element that a recipe on a tablet or TV show can't have. Reading a tablet in the bathtub is a little more risky than reading a book. But this goes beyond the physical object for me. I think of a recipe as a little snapshot of what I've experienced, and putting them together in a book is like collating a personal culinary diary.

It's a time-consuming process, but I love every part of it, from the research, recipe development, and writing about my personal stories to the photo shoot, where the book begins to take a visual shape. Writing a book may start off as a solitary activity, but the more the book progresses, the more essential it is to work with people you admire and find inspiring (more about them in the Acknowledgments). They all play a part in pushing me as a food writer and making the book the best it can be.

My ideas start with a taste, a flavor, and a sketch in my kitchen notebook, then evolve from experiments in my kitchen back into the book, and eventually (I hope!) to your kitchen and mouth. My culinary holy grail is to find my cookbook on your bookshelf with greasy fingerprints, food-stain splatters, and your own personal scribbles on the recipes.

This book is a collection of recipes that were inspired by my travels, adventures, and food experiences, which I hope will, ultimately, inspire you to cook!

Rachel x

Cream of tomato soup with crunchy lemon chickpeas

Starters

Olive Oil

Light bites or small dishes to tantalize your taste buds, that's what starters are all about. More often than not they set a tone, showing your guests what culinary delights await and giving diners a little taste of what's in store. Starters also make a fantastic meal for one or two—see my Little Socca Cakes with Ratatouille (page 33) or my Hot Butter and Soy Sauce Mackerel with Chopped Salad (page 41). I often opt for a selection of starters rather than one main course when I eat out. I'm never happy with just one plate of food; I like to try lots of different things—and with small dishes I can leave the restaurant without feeling like I need a forklift to take me home. Since I began developing recipes for a living, I often also find myself having a starter as a lunch or light dinner, and sometimes even for breakfast ... or perhaps that's just my Asian heritage coming to light.

Starters aren't just reserved for special occasions. In Europe it is perfectly normal, and totally sensible, in my mind, to kick off a home meal—guests or no guests, midweek or brunch—with a little appetite whetter; it's a great way of prolonging time spent at the table too. When I cooked for a French family, I discovered that a starter can simply be a slice of perfectly ripe melon with a few ribbons of salty, sweet Bayonne ham. For some other easy, quick starters, see my Poached Fennel with Pink Prawns and Toasted Almonds (page 38), Pan Con Tomate (page 25), or the rather unusual Morcilla, Egg, and Crisps (page 25).

I don't believe you need to serve something complex in order to wow your guests, but if you're looking to push the boat out then some of my favorites are my ultra-bling Smörgåstårta (page 57) or my dainty Baked Goat's Cheese Cigars with Melon, Radish, and Cucumber Slaw (page 21).

And if you're new to the kitchen, or have a tendency to burn your food, I even have a recipe for you too: my Burnt Leek Parcels with Romesco Sauce (page 34). It's one of those few recipes in which burning your food is not so much undesirable as a sought-after outcome.

Creamy mushroom soup with bouncy dill fish balls

Serves
4

Preparation time:
25 minutes

Cooking time:
30 minutes

The archipelago around Stockholm, with its crystal-clear water, crisp fresh air, and untouched scenery, captured what for me is the essence of Sweden. It is the juxtaposition of water and forest that inspired this recipe, and, of course, the Swedes' love of meatballs. I turned tradition on its head a little, and let the coast inspire these fish balls. But these aren't just any old fish balls.

Instead of taking the more traditional Swedish approach to making meatballs (ground meat or fish, rolled into a ball), I've taken inspiration from my Chinese heritage. I love the chewy texture of Chinese fish balls, which is created by slapping the flesh around. I've spotted old ladies in fish markets in Malaysia doing this. The pounding and slamming of the fish stretches and uncoils the previously wound protein strands, which makes for this unusual bouncy texture.

For the fish balls

14 oz cod or pollack loin, skinned and deboned

2 tbsp chopped fresh dill

½ tsp sea salt

¼ tsp white pepper

For the soup

1 tbsp olive oil

2 knobs of butter

2 onions, peeled and finely chopped

2 cloves of garlic, peeled and minced

2 sprigs of thyme

1 lb portobello mushrooms, roughly chopped

sea salt and freshly ground black pepper

2 cups good-quality beef stock

1¼ cups heavy cream

1 knob of butter

2 oz wild mushrooms (such as chanterelles), brushed clean and torn if large

juice and zest of 1 unwaxed lemon

2 to 3 knäckebröd (rye crispbread)

chopped fresh dill for garnish

To make the fish balls: Pat the fish dry with a clean kitchen towel. In a food processor, blend the fish to a smooth paste with the dill, salt, and white pepper. Add about 3 tbsp water and keep blending. Check the consistency and add as much water as needed to bind into a paste; you want it to be pastelike but not too wet to form into balls.

Now it's time to start slapping your fish. Take the mixture in your hands and keep slapping it down on a clean work surface for a minute or two. As the mixture is thrown down more and more, you will notice a bounce develop in the texture.

Divide the mixture into 16 portions and shape into small balls. If you find it easier, wet your palms before rolling the mixture into neat balls. Place on a clean plate.

To make the soup: Heat the oil and butter in a large saucepan over low heat. Add the onions, garlic, thyme, and mushrooms. Season with salt and black pepper and cook, uncovered, for 15 minutes, or until soft.

Add the stock to the mushrooms, bring to a simmer, and let simmer, uncovered, for 10 minutes. Add the cream. Remove and discard the thyme. Using an immersion blender, blend the soup until smooth.

Fill a medium saucepan with water, bring it to a boil, and drop in the fish balls to cook for 3 minutes, or until they float to the top. Remove with a slotted spoon and set aside.

Heat the butter in a frying pan over medium-high heat. Add the wild mushrooms and sauté for 2 to 3 minutes, then set aside.

Finish the soup by stirring in the lemon juice and tasting for seasoning. Ladle the soup into bowls, adding four fish balls to each. Garnish with some shards of knäckebröd as croutons, fresh dill, and the lemon zest. Scatter some of the sautéed mushrooms over the soup in each bowl before serving.

Tip

Soak the bowl of your blender or food processor immediately after making the fish paste, as it has a tendency to stick!

Get ahead

You can make the soup a day before. The fish balls can be formed the day before serving. Store in an airtight container and cook just before serving.

Cream of tomato soup with crunchy lemon chickpeas

Serves	Preparation time:	Cooking time:
4 as a starter	15 minutes	35 to 45 minutes

Anyone who has ever cooked and eaten on a budget in the United Kingdom will be familiar with some of Britain's perennial foodstuffs: canned soup and tomatoey baked beans. They were the standby meals of choice back in my university days, and there is nothing quite like a cream of tomato soup to brighten up a winter night.

I love these lemony chickpeas (I always have a can of chickpeas on hand in the cupboard); they're my version of croutons. I like to sprinkle them on top of soups, but they are equally delicious as a stand-in for nuts—a homemade bar snack.

one 14-oz can chickpeas, drained and rinsed

1 unwaxed lemon, sliced

4 cloves of garlic, unpeeled

1 tbsp canola or other vegetable oil

sea salt

one 28-oz can good-quality cherry tomatoes

1 cup vegetable stock or water

1 tsp sugar

1 tbsp red wine vinegar

freshly ground pepper

¾ cup heavy cream

Preheat the oven to 350°F.

Combine the chickpeas, lemon slices, garlic, and oil in a small bowl and toss to coat. Place the chickpeas on a rimmed baking sheet. Sprinkle with salt and roast for 30 to 40 minutes, or until golden and crunchy.

Meanwhile, put the tomatoes and stock in a medium saucepan and bring to a simmer. Remove the roasted garlic from the baking sheet and squeeze the garlic from its papery husks, then add to the saucepan and simmer for 5 minutes. Add the sugar and vinegar and continue simmering for 1 minute. Taste for salt and pepper and stir in half the cream, then remove from the heat and use an immersion blender to blend until smooth.

Ladle the soup into bowls and garnish with the crunchy chickpeas, a slice of roasted lemon, and a drizzle of the remaining cream.

Tip
Don't boil the soup with the cream in it, as it will curdle.

Baked goat's cheese cigars with melon, radish, and cucumber slaw

Serves 4 as a starter	Preparation time: 20 minutes	Cooking time: 15 to 20 minutes

The Nice area in France tends to produce goat's cheese rather than cheese made from cow's milk, as the landscape is too rugged and rough for cows to graze. Eating goat's cheese from this region really captures the flavors of the terroir. Goats graze on whatever grows, from wild herbs, such as oregano and thyme, to berries, and these flavors subtly influence the end product. These cigars make a delectable summer starter or an aperitif with a glass of rosé, showcasing the flavors of Provence.

For the cigars

1 to 2 rectangular filo sheets (depending on the size of your sheets)

4 tbsp butter, melted

leaves from 8 sprigs of thyme

4½ oz soft goat's cheese

4 tsp honey (lavender, if possible)

For the slaw

1 small cucumber or ½ regular cucumber

½ unripe galia melon, seeded

6 radishes, trimmed and sliced into thin rounds

For the dressing

1 tbsp extra-virgin olive oil

½ tbsp red wine vinegar

sea salt and freshly ground pepper

To make the cigars: Preheat the oven to 350°F. Line a baking sheet with parchment paper.

Unroll a sheet of filo horizontally on your work surface. Cut the filo sheet in half lengthwise and in half crosswise to make four rectangles measuring about 6 by 8 in. Lay them all out on the work surface, then brush the rectangles generously with the butter, reserving about 1 tbsp to brush the tops.

Sprinkle some thyme leaves along the long length of each pastry and fold it in about ¾ in to encase them. Crumble the goat's cheese in a line along the opposite short side of the pastry. Drizzle the honey along the goat's cheese on each pastry. Starting at the goat's cheese end, roll the pastry over the cheese and all the way to the thyme, pressing gently to seal. Repeat the process to make four cigars. Place on the prepared baking sheet and brush with the remaining butter. Bake for 15 to 20 minutes, or until golden and crisp.

To make the slaw: Using a mandoline or speed peeler, julienne the cucumber and the melon flesh. Place them in a bowl and add the radishes.

To make the dressing: Combine the ingredients in a jam jar and shake to mix well.

Once the cigars are baked, toss the slaw with the dressing and place in the center of each plate. Serve with the cigars on top.

Tips

Filo sheets dry out quickly. Be sure to store them in plastic wrap. Be gentle when brushing the sheets, as they can tear easily.

You can flavor the goat's cheese with any dried herbs or spices, such as cayenne pepper, smoked paprika, ground cumin, or chile. Or try your favorite chutney or caramelized onions in place of the honey.

Speedy chorizo and chickpea stew

Serves
4 to 6 as a starter
or 2 as a main

Preparation time:
10 minutes

Cooking time:
20 minutes

One of the great things about tapas is that they can be whipped up in a flash. This speedy little stew is at home on a table laden with a selection of tapas, or served as a tasty meal for two that can be ready in minutes.

8 green onions

1 tbsp olive oil

1 tbsp finely chopped fresh rosemary leaves

1 tsp smoked sweet paprika

one 15-oz can chickpeas, drained and rinsed

2 chorizo sausages

2 tbsp sherry vinegar

one 15-oz can tomatoes

sea salt and freshly ground pepper

Chop the green onions into rounds, separating the white and green parts. Put the oil into a large frying pan over high heat. Add the white parts of the green onions, the rosemary, smoked paprika, and chickpeas to the pan and fry for 2 minutes.

Slice the chorizo into ⅛-in-thick rounds, add to the pan, and cook for 2 minutes. Add the sherry vinegar, turn down the heat, and cook gently, uncovered, stirring occasionally, for 5 minutes.

Add the tomatoes and cook for 10 minutes. Taste for salt and pepper and adjust if necessary.

Finish the stew with the green tops of the green onions, sprinkling them over just before serving.

Morcilla, egg, and crisps

Serves	Preparation time:	Cooking time:
4	2 minutes	10 minutes

Okay, so it sounds a little out there, but this tasty tapa is not as crazy as you might think. Unlike the British relationship with crisps (potato chips), which might involve a stop by the corner shop for a sneaky bag of Walker's, there's a long-standing tradition of handmade, freshly fried crisps in Spain. I ate this dish in a tapas bar in Barcelona; I loved the idea that you can pimp up a bag of potato chips, so I have re-created it here.

one 2-oz bag salted potato chips

5 oz morcilla (blood sausage), casing removed

1 tbsp olive or canola oil

3 eggs

Empty the bag of chips into a serving dish.

Roughly crumble or chop the morcilla. Heat a large nonstick frying pan over high heat and dry-fry the morcilla for 3 to 4 minutes, until cooked through. Scatter the sausage over the chips.

Add the oil to the frying pan, heat, and crack the eggs in one by one. Cook for 2 to 3 minutes, until the whites are set but the yolks are still runny (put a lid or plate over the pan to speed it up).

Using a spatula, gently place the fried eggs over the morcilla and serve.

Pan con tomate

Serves	Preparation time:	Cooking time:
4	10 minutes	5 minutes

This is my take on the classic tomato on bread that is ubiquitous in Spanish wine and tapas bars. This is possibly one of the simplest tapas you'll find, but I have jazzed mine up with a herby and garlicky butter.

4 large slices sourdough bread

10½ oz heirloom tomatoes

1½ oz fresh basil, or whatever herbs you like

2 cloves of garlic, peeled

6 tbsp salted butter

sea salt and freshly ground pepper

pinch of sweet smoked paprika (optional)

Grill or toast the bread on both sides. Thinly slice the tomatoes.

In a small blender or by hand, very finely chop the basil and garlic and mix together. Melt the butter in a small saucepan and add the herbs and garlic to it. Add a pinch of salt and pepper and remove from the heat before the butter browns.

Pile the tomatoes high onto the toasted bread and drizzle with the hot garlic-herb butter. Finish with a sprinkle of sweet smoked paprika, if desired, before serving.

A couple of small plates of food and a bunch of friends is my favorite way to relax.

Razor clams with tzatziki and pomegranate

Serves
4 as a canapé or starter

Preparation time:
10 minutes

Cooking time:
30 seconds

Whenever there are starters being served in Turkey, a small dish of tzatziki is likely to appear. It's a simple blend of cucumber, garlic, and creamy yogurt, but each family and restaurant will have their own secret method and ratio, making it their signature.

In my view, the perfect tzatziki is made using a crunchy Lebanese or ridge cucumber with the seeds scooped out; salting it in a colander also draws out the moisture. Pomegranate seeds are the perfect way to elevate any dish, savory or sweet, and they add an exceedingly satisfying crunch.

8 razor clams

½ lemon

5 tbsp Greek yogurt

I small clove of garlic, peeled and minced

pinch of sea salt

½ Lebanese cucumber or ridge cucumber, peeled

¼ cup pomegranate seeds

Bring a large saucepan of water to a boil. Set up a large bowl of iced water nearby. Drop 4 razor clams into the boiling water, then fish them out almost immediately with a pair of tongs and drop them straight into the iced water. They should open but not cook. Repeat with the remaining clams.

Pull the clams out of their shells and use a pair of scissors to cut the black sac out of the clam, remove the "beak," then chop the clams into thumbnail-size pieces. Put the clams into a bowl and squeeze a little lemon juice over the top. Wash and dry 8 half-shells and set aside.

Mix together the yogurt, garlic, salt, and a squeeze of lemon. Place in a disposable piping bag or ziplock bag and snip off the end.

Cut the cucumber in half lengthwise and scoop out the seeds. Cut into fine julienne strips on a mandoline or by hand.

Put 3 or 4 dollops of the garlic yogurt along a half-shell. Put the clam pieces in between the yogurt. Garnish with cucumber and scatter some of the pomegranate seeds over the top. Repeat with the remaining half-shells and serve.

Tip

A good way to tell if your clams are fresh is to tickle the foot, which should retract right away; if there is no sign of life, don't buy them.

Razor clams with crispy rice and hot sauce

Serves
4 as a canapé or starter

Preparation time:
30 minutes

Cooking time:
30 minutes

On the Princes' Islands in Turkey, seafood is a staple. *Midye dolma*—mussels stuffed with rice, pine nuts, currants, and spices—are sold on the beachfront, and they served as the inspiration for this little mezze of mine. "Mezze" means taste, flavor, snack, or relish, which is how these are intended to be offered—as tastes, alongside other little dishes. But don't think you have to make lots of complicated dishes for a successful spread; simply using one main ingredient and varying it with some sides or garnishes is a less fussy solution. This stuffed-clam recipe pairs perfectly with Razor Clams with Tzatziki and Pomegranate (page 29).

8 razor clams

2 tbsp olive oil, plus more for drizzling

1 small onion, peeled and finely chopped

4 cloves of garlic, peeled and finely minced

8 cherry tomatoes, roughly chopped

1 small red chile, seeded and finely chopped

1 tbsp red wine vinegar

½ cup cooked brown rice

1 small red Romano pepper, seeded and finely chopped

1 tbsp dried mint

2 sprigs of parsley

Heat a grill.

Bring a large saucepan of water to a boil. Set up a large bowl of iced water nearby. Drop 4 razor clams into the boiling water, then fish them out almost immediately with a pair of tongs and drop them straight into the iced water. They should open but not cook. Repeat with the remaining clams.

Pull the clams out of their shells and use a pair of scissors to cut the black sack out of the clam, remove the "beak," then chop the clams into thumbnail-size pieces. Put the clams into a bowl. Wash and dry 8 half-shells and set aside.

Put 1 tbsp of the oil into a large nonstick frying pan over medium heat. Add the onion, garlic, tomatoes, and chile and fry for about 15 minutes, or until the tomatoes and onion are soft but not brown. Transfer the tomato mixture to a quart-size liquid measuring cup and, using an immersion blender, blend into a smooth paste. Stir in the vinegar.

Wipe out the frying pan and place over medium heat. Add the remaining 1 tbsp oil. Add the brown rice and fry for about 10 minutes, or until golden and crisp. Add the clams for the last couple of minutes.

Spread some of the sauce on the bottom of a half-shell, followed by some of the crispy rice and clams and Romano pepper pieces. Sprinkle with the dried mint and parsley and drizzle with olive oil. Repeat with the remaining half-shells, and serve.

Little socca cakes with ratatouille

Serves	Preparation time:	Cooking time:
4 as a starter	20 minutes	1¼ hours

In Brittany they have crêpes and *galettes* (buckwheat pancakes), but in Nice they have *socca*. It's a sort of pancake made from chickpea flour, which is baked in a wood-fired oven and has a crispy, slightly blistered, charred crust. At home it's a little difficult to re-create that smoky flavor (unless you happen to have a wood-fired oven), but these are worth making nevertheless.

For the ratatouille

2 cloves of garlic, peeled and minced

1 onion, peeled and finely chopped

1 tsp fresh thyme leaves

3 tbsp olive oil

1 eggplant, thinly sliced

1 small zucchini, thinly sliced

1 yellow bell pepper, thinly sliced

6 tomatoes, quartered

pinch of sugar

sea salt

For the anchovy sauce

10 anchovies in olive oil

2 tbsp extra-virgin olive oil or oil from the anchovies

zest and juice of ½ unwaxed lemon

2 Tbsp water

For the socca

1⅔ cups chickpea flour

1 tsp dried oregano

1 tsp sea salt

3 tbsp olive oil, plus more for frying

1 cup water

To make the ratatouille: Preheat the oven to 350°F.

In a frying pan over medium-high heat, gently sauté the garlic, onion, and thyme in 2 tbsp of the oil. Once the onion is translucent and soft, add the eggplant and cook for 5 minutes, or until soft.

Toss the remaining vegetables in a large roasting pan with the remaining 1 tbsp oil, the sugar, and a little salt. Add the cooked onion and eggplant and mix them together. Cover the pan with aluminum foil or parchment paper, then bake for 1 hour.

Meanwhile, to make the anchovy sauce: In a food processor, blend together the anchovies, oil, lemon zest, lemon juice, and water. (The sauce should be the consistency of heavy cream, so add a little more water if necessary.) Set aside.

To make the socca: Whisk the chickpea flour, oregano, and salt with the oil and water. Put 1 tsp oil into a nonstick frying pan over medium-high heat, then ladle about 3 tbsp of batter into a circle, creating a 3-in-diameter pancake. Cook for 1 minute on each side, or until golden. Repeat with the rest of the batter.

Divide the socca among plates, adding a generous heap of ratatouille, followed by a drizzle of the anchovy sauce.

Tip
Be sure to get the pan nice and hot for the socca.

Get ahead
The socca and ratatouille can be cooled and kept wrapped in plastic wrap in the refrigerator for up to 2 days. Reheat in a 325°F oven for 20 minutes.

Burnt leek parcels with romesco sauce

Serves
4

Preparation time:
15 minutes

Cooking time:
25 to 30 minutes

Pass the parcel was one of my favorite party games as a kid. Who says you can't play it as a grown-up? This recipe is all about wrapping up some Catalonian flavors, and letting your guests unpack the surprise. Burning the leeks adds a slight smokiness, and for those who are deft at burning things in the kitchen, this one is for you. The burnt parts are peeled off to reveal the juicy, sweet, and tender leek underneath—perfect for dunking into the nutty, fresh romesco sauce. During springtime it's a Catalan tradition to serve romesco sauce with young spring onions, or *calçots*, which work in a similar way to leeks in this recipe.

3 red bell peppers, halved and seeded

½ cup pine nuts

1 clove of garlic, peeled

4 tbsp extra-virgin olive oil

⅓ cup fresh bread crumbs

½ tsp sweet smoked paprika

1 tbsp sherry vinegar

sea salt

juice of ½ unwaxed lemon

12 leeks

Preheat the broiler. Place the bell peppers skin-side up on an oiled baking sheet and broil for 3 to 5 minutes, or until black and tender. Place in a plastic bag and let steam for about 20 minutes. When cool enough to handle, remove and discard the skins and set the flesh aside.

Toast the pine nuts in a small frying pan over medium heat, shaking continuously for about 3 minutes, or until golden. Tip them onto a plate to cool. When cool, place them in a blender or food processor with the broiled peppers, garlic, olive oil, and bread crumbs. Pulse until smooth, then add the paprika and sherry vinegar. Season the romesco with salt and lemon juice if necessary.

Lay the leeks about ½ in apart on a baking sheet (you may have to do this in batches). Broil for about 8 minutes, or until blackened, turning them every couple of minutes. Wrap 3 leeks in a piece of newspaper to make a parcel, then repeat with the remaining leeks so that you have four bundles. They will steam in the paper until ready to serve.

Place the romesco in a bowl and let everyone open up their own parcel, peeling away the burnt outer leaves, then dunking the soft, sweet interior straight into the sauce.

Tips

Try using Spanish Marcona almonds instead of pine nuts. They are often sold salted, so check the seasoning before adding salt to the sauce.

You may play around with the consistency of this sauce by altering the quantity of olive oil; use it as a dressing or as a paste for crostini.

Get ahead

The romesco sauce will keep well in the refrigerator for up to 3 days.

Beet oatcakes with chicken liver parfait

Serves	Preparation time:	Cooking time:	Resting time:
4	40 minutes	40 minutes	2 hours minimum

This recipe is loosely inspired by the phenomenal "meat fruit" at Heston Blumenthal's London restaurant, Dinner. The most perfectly glossy mandarin arrives at the table, which you cut open to reveal a silky chicken liver and foie gras parfait.

For the chicken liver parfait

¼ cup salted butter

1 shallot, peeled and thinly sliced

2 cloves of garlic, peeled and crushed

2 sprigs of thyme

4½ oz chicken livers, trimmed

1 tbsp brandy

½ tsp sea salt

¼ tsp finely ground pepper

For the jelly

one ¾-oz gelatin leaf

⅓ cup orange juice

1 tbsp sugar

1 small orange or clementine

For the oatcakes

½ beet

6 tbsp rolled oats

½ cup plus 1 tbsp all-purpose flour

½ tsp baking powder

½ tsp sea salt

½ tbsp sugar

¼ cup unsalted butter, melted and cooled

To make the chicken liver parfait: Melt a small knob of the butter in a large saucepan over low heat and add the shallot, garlic, and thyme. Cook for 5 minutes, or until the shallot has softened but hasn't browned. Increase the heat to medium-high and add the livers and brandy, then cook for about 2 minutes on each side, or until the livers have browned but are still slightly pink in the middle. Let cool for 5 minutes. Remove the thyme.

Transfer the mixture to a food processor or blender and add the remaining butter and the salt and pepper. Divide the parfait mixture between small jars or ramekins and smooth the tops with a spoon. Leave in the refrigerator for up to 2 days.

To make the jelly: Soak the gelatin leaf in cold water for 5 to 10 minutes. Pour the orange juice and sugar into a saucepan over medium-high heat. Heat until the sugar has dissolved. Squeeze the gelatin leaf and pour away the water. Strain the orange juice through a sieve directly over the gelatin leaf. Stir to dissolve.

Peel the orange with a paring knife, removing all the pith, and slice into thin rounds. Top the chicken liver parfait with an orange round, then pour the jelly on top. Return the parfaits to the refrigerator to set for at least 2 hours but preferably overnight.

To make the oatcakes: Preheat the oven to 325°F. Peel and finely grate the beet into a bowl. Add the oats, flour, baking powder, salt, and sugar. Mix well, then add the melted butter and bring together to form a ball.

Roll out with a rolling pin between two sheets of parchment paper to 1½ to 2 in thick. Cut into rounds using a 2-in cookie cutter and put on a parchment-lined baking sheet. Roll out the leftover dough and cut out more rounds, so that you have 16 oatcakes in total. Bake for 25 to 30 minutes, then let cool on a rack.

Serve the oatcakes on a platter, with the parfait alongside for spreading.

Poached fennel with pink prawns and toasted almonds

Serves
4

Preparation time:
10 minutes

Cooking time:
15 minutes

In my line of work I eat countless different dishes, and it's often pretty impossible to keep track of all those flavors. However, some memories stick with me. Grandma's cake, Mum's roast, or a birthday dish are the easy ones to recall, but sometimes it can be the more unassuming dishes that make the biggest impact. The memory of eating fennel poached in milk at a friend's house in Milan many years ago is something that has stuck with me ever since. The lightly fragrant creamy broth with the tender fennel was divine. My recipe might have a few extras, but the hero is still the simple poached fennel.

I large bulb of fennel or 2 small ones

¾ cup whole milk

7 tbsp heavy cream

¾ cup vegetable stock, heated

pinch of sea salt

pinch of white pepper

5½ oz raw peeled king prawns, heads removed

¼ cup sliced almonds

zest of I unwaxed lemon

extra-virgin olive oil for drizzling

Quarter the fennel lengthwise. Remove the fronds, setting them aside for later. Trim the toughest tips of the stalks and remove any scruffy outer leaves. Place the fennel quarters in a medium saucepan (the fennel should fit snugly) and add the milk, cream, stock, salt, and pepper.

Bring the liquid to a gentle boil, cover, and cook over low heat for 15 minutes, or until the fennel is tender, adding the prawns during the final 3 to 4 minutes of cooking. Remove from the heat and check the seasoning.

In the meantime, toast the almonds in a dry skillet, tossing until golden, I to 2 minutes.

Place the wedges of poached fennel in shallow bowls and divide the prawns among them. Pour over some of the hot poaching liquid, then sprinkle with the toasted almonds and the fennel fronds. Scatter the lemon zest on top and drizzle with olive oil before serving.

Tips
Don't let the broth come to a boil or it might curdle.

You may use cooked prawns instead of raw; just add them for the final minute of cooking.

Get ahead
You can cook the fennel in advance and reheat it over low heat until warmed through. Raw fennel will discolor, however, if prepped ahead without cooking.

Hot butter and soy sauce mackerel with chopped salad

Serves	Preparation time:	Cooking time:
4 as a starter	15 minutes	5 minutes

Istanbul lies half in Europe and half in Asia and that fusion has influenced the local food greatly, just like the Asian soy sauce and European butter that sit together happily in this dish.

Mackerel is everywhere in Istanbul, whether it's at the fish market, so fresh it's still flopping around, or being cooked on a hot grill at a street food stand. It's cheap, very nutritious, and rich in omega-3.

½ cup unsalted butter

For the salad

2 tbsp white wine vinegar

½ red onion, peeled and thinly sliced

1 small Lebanese cucumber or ½ hothouse cucumber, peeled

5 tomatoes, quartered

1 tbsp finely chopped fresh dill

pinch of sea salt

1 tbsp pomegranate molasses

2 tsp chopped fresh thyme leaves

1 tsp dried mint

4 mackerel fillets, deboned with skin left on

2 tbsp light soy sauce or tamari

Heat the butter in a saucepan over low heat until melted. Let it simmer gently until the foam rises to the top. Once the butter stops sputtering and no more foam seems to be rising to the surface, remove the pan from the heat and skim off the foam with a spoon.

Line a mesh sieve with cheesecloth and set the sieve over a bowl. Carefully pour the warm butter through the sieve into the bowl, leaving behind any solids from the bottom of the pan. Discard the milk solids left in the cheesecloth.

To make the salad: Put the vinegar in a small bowl, add the red onion, and leave to soak. Seed the cucumber, cut into small cubes, and put in a large bowl. Add the tomatoes and dill, sprinkle with the salt, and mix together. Add the onion and pomegranate molasses. Toss well.

Mix together the thyme leaves and dried mint. Heat a large non-stick frying pan and add 1 tbsp of the clarified butter to the pan. When the pan is smoking hot, add the mackerel fillets, skin-side down. Cook for 2 minutes before turning over and cooking for 2 minutes more.

Add the soy sauce to the remaining clarified butter. Drizzle the fish with the sauce and sprinkle with the herb mix.

Serve the mackerel on a bed of salad. Drizzle a spoonful of the cooking juices over each mackerel fillet.

Tip

If you can't find pomegranate molasses, use a mixture of lemon juice and honey instead.

English garden salad

Serves	Preparation time:	Cooking time:
4	45 minutes	30 minutes

I love a salad, and I often wish salads got a little bit more attention as the highlight of a meal. They are all too often seen as diet food, carelessly pulled from a bag and tossed with a bottled dressing, but that's not how it's done in my home.

Making a great salad is all about being creative with your presentation. Don't just slice or chop; play around with dicing, making ribbons or batons. Different textures and temperatures are also key to a great salad. Crunchy, soft, creamy, hot, and cold; don't be afraid to mix it up as I have with my English garden salad.

I tsp granulated sugar

6 tbsp white wine vinegar

2 tbsp water

I red onion, peeled and thinly sliced

2 potatoes, peeled and cut into ½-in cubes

8 slices smoked bacon, finely chopped

I small cucumber or ½ hothouse cucumber

1¼ cups cottage cheese (see page 246 or storebought)

½ cup crème fraîche or Greek yogurt

I small bunch chives, finely chopped

pinch of sea salt

½ tsp freshly ground pepper

8 radishes, thinly sliced

2 handfuls of fresh peas

2 handfuls of salad leaves, washed

In a small bowl, dissolve the sugar in the vinegar and water. Add half the onion to the bowl and mix.

Place the cubes of potato in a medium saucepan. Cover with salted cold water, bring to a boil, then simmer for about 5 minutes, or until just tender when pierced with the tip of a knife. Drain.

Put the bacon in a large nonstick frying pan over medium heat. Fry for 2 minutes, then add the other half of the onion and cook for 10 minutes. Add the potatoes and cook for 5 to 7 minutes, or until all the ingredients are lightly golden, stirring occasionally so everything browns evenly.

Meanwhile, with a peeler, cut ribbons from half of the cucumber. Cut the other half into small cubes.

In a small bowl, mix the cottage cheese with the crème fraîche, chives, salt, and pepper. Taste and add more seasoning if desired. Drain the pickling liquid from the onion.

Spread the cottage cheese mixture on plates. Divide the hot potato-bacon mixture among the plates, followed by the cubes and ribbons of cucumber, the radish slices, peas, and salad leaves. Place some of the pickled onion on top, and serve immediately.

Bean salad

Serves 4 as a side	Preparation time: 10 minutes	Soaking time: 8 hours	Cooking time: 1 to 1½ hours

Dried pulses and beans (chickpeas, lentils, and pod beans) seem to be among those items that are bought on a spur-of-the-moment health whim, but then lie forgotten at the back of the cupboard for a couple of years.

Blow off the dust and make a delicious dish like this navy bean salad. It's cheap and nutritious, and makes a surprisingly tasty alternative to standard roast potatoes as a side dish for my Provençal roast chicken (see page 105).

1 cup dried navy beans

2 tbsp red wine vinegar

3 tbsp extra-virgin olive oil

pinch of sea salt

pinch of granulated sugar

1 small red onion, peeled and finely chopped

1 handful chopped chives

freshly ground pepper

Soak the beans in a large bowl of cold water overnight, or for about 8 hours. Drain the beans and place in a large saucepan with plenty of cold water to cover. Bring to a boil, skimming off any scum that rises to the surface, and cook for 1 to 1½ hours, adding more just-boiled water to cover if necessary. When the beans are tender, drain in a colander and set aside.

In a large serving bowl, whisk together the vinegar, oil, salt, and sugar. Add the red onion and the warm beans and toss to coat well.

Sprinkle with the chives and pepper, and serve.

Tips

The salad can be made up to 2 days in advance and served at room temperature.

When seeing if the beans are cooked, check a few, as they can cook at different speeds.

If you don't have time to soak the beans, canned beans are a good alternative. Rinse them well before using. However, when tossing them in the dressing, do so gently as they tend to be softer than the home-cooked variety. The equivalent quantity for this recipe is about two 15-oz cans or one 28-oz can of beans.

Roasted cauliflower and caraway salad

Serves	Preparation time:	Cooking time:
4 as a side or starter	10 minutes	25 to 30 minutes

Having spent my teenage years in Bavaria, I have had plenty of cabbage and caraway salads in my life, as they're served at each and every beer festival. But cabbage isn't the only thing that goes particularly well with caraway: cauliflower works too.

I small head of cauliflower, trimmed and separated into bite-size florets

I tbsp olive oil

sea salt

2½ tbsp apple cider vinegar

½ tsp granulated sugar

½ tsp brown mustard

2 tsp caraway seeds

6 slices smoked bacon, finely chopped

I small red onion, peeled and finely sliced

I unpeeled apple, cored and sliced

small handful of finely chopped fresh chives

Preheat the oven to 400°F.

Toss the cauliflower florets in the oil and a pinch of salt. Place on a baking sheet and roast in the oven for 20 to 25 minutes, or until golden.

In the meantime, whisk together the vinegar, sugar, and mustard in a bowl. Dry-fry the caraway seeds in a frying pan over medium-high heat until aromatic and add to the bowl, then return the pan to the heat.

Place the bacon and onion in the pan and fry for about 5 minutes, or until the bacon is crisp and cooked through. Transfer to a salad bowl, then throw in the roasted cauliflower and the apple, and mix. Pour the dressing over and toss everything together. Taste for salt and sprinkle the chives over the top. This dish can be served warm or cold.

Tips

You can use thinly sliced raw green cabbage instead of the cauliflower.

If you aren't a fan of caraway, try fennel or cumin seeds instead.

You may leave the onion raw if you prefer. Finely slice it and add it to the vinaigrette to soak for a few minutes before assembling the salad.

Get ahead

You can make this salad a day in advance, leave it in the refrigerator, and serve at room temperature. You could also reheat it in the oven at 325°F for 15 minutes.

Panzanella

Serves
4

Preparation time:
40 minutes

Salting time:
30 minutes

Cooking time:
15 minutes

Stuffed with the sunny flavors of the Amalfi Coast—roasted eggplant and tomatoes, dressed with a zingy caper and basil sauce—this is my take on the fantastic Italian bread salad. Panzanella is a great way to use up stale bread. When paired with tomatoes, it soaks up all the lovely juices and oil, giving it a new lease of life.

For the eggplant

2 small eggplant

3 tbsp sea salt

1½ cups water

½ cup plus 2 tbsp white wine vinegar

¼ cup granulated sugar

2 tbsp olive oil

For the basil and caper sauce

6 tbsp extra-virgin olive oil

2 tbsp lemon juice

1 small clove of garlic, peeled

1 small bunch of fresh basil, leaves and stalks

1 tbsp capers, rinsed

sea salt

1 large round loaf white sourdough bread

1 tbsp olive oil

1 lb heirloom tomatoes, a mix of colors, quartered or halved if small

7 oz buffalo mozzarella, drained and torn

To make the eggplant: Trim the stems off the eggplant and cut them lengthwise into ⅛-in-thick slices. Sprinkle generously with the salt and place in a colander in the sink for about 30 minutes. Rinse and pat dry with a kitchen towel.

Place the water, vinegar, and sugar in a large saucepan and bring to a simmer, allowing the sugar to dissolve. Blanch the eggplant slices in the liquid for 2 minutes or until just tender. Do this in two batches if necessary. Remove the eggplant with a slotted spoon and place in a colander to cool. Pat with paper towels to absorb any excess water.

Put a griddle pan over high heat. Brush both sides of the eggplant slices with the oil. When the griddle pan is smoking hot, sear the eggplant slices in batches for about 1 minute on each side, and set aside.

To make the basil and caper sauce: In a food processor, blend together the oil, lemon juice, garlic, basil, and capers, until you have a nice green sauce. Season with salt.

Trim the top off the bread using a bread knife. Set the lid aside and scoop out the insides of the bread, right to the crust. Tear the insides into bite-size pieces. (Reserve half to use for something else at a later date; they freeze well.)

Heat the oil in a frying pan and, when hot, add the torn-up bread and fry for 2 to 3 minutes, or until golden brown. Place in a bowl with the tomatoes and toss together with the basil and caper sauce.

Arrange a generous layer of eggplant slices on the base of the bread. Add a layer of mozzarella, then one of tomatoes and bread, and continue to layer the ingredients, making sure to press them into the bread bowl firmly to fit in as many as possible.

Place the lid on the bread bowl, wrap tightly in plastic wrap, and set aside for a few hours, or up to overnight. Remove the plastic wrap and cut into thick slices to serve.

Tip

Marinate any leftover eggplant in olive oil, salt, chopped chile, garlic, and parsley. When fully submerged in a sterilized jar stored in the refrigerator, it should keep for a week.

Chilled cucumber soup

Serves	Preparation time:	Resting time:
4	15 minutes	15 minutes minimum

Inspiration for a recipe can come to me anywhere, and this one, rather bizarrely, was inspired by a skiing trip to St. Moritz. The land of rich and heavy fondues is the least likely place you would associate with a summery chilled cucumber soup. I, however, had the most amazing gin and tonic in the après-ski hours. The barman asked me whether I would like to have some pepper in it—a first for me. That hit of pepper with the juniper flavors of the gin and slice of cucumber was a revelation. I wanted to replicate that flavor combination in a dish, and came up with this vibrant and refreshing soup.

10 juniper berries

sea salt

2 large cucumbers

4 stalks celery, leaves left on

1 to 2 tbsp white wine vinegar

¼ cup crème fraîche

white pepper

Grind the juniper berries with 1 tsp salt into a fine powder in a spice grinder or using a pestle and mortar. Cut a 3-in length off one cucumber and set it aside. Coarsely chop the remainder of the cucumber, along with the celery. Place the chopped cucumber and celery in a blender, along with the vinegar, and blend until as smooth as possible, blending in batches if necessary.

Line a sieve with cheesecloth and place over a medium bowl. Pour the blended celery and cucumber through the cheesecloth, again in batches if necessary. Gather the corners of the cheesecloth and twist to squeeze out all the juice into the bowl. Pour the juice from the bowl into a pitcher and place in the refrigerator until ice cold, at least 30 minutes, or the freezer for 15 minutes.

Transfer the pulp from the cheesecloth to a bowl and mix with the crème fraîche and the ground juniper berries. Taste for salt, then put into the refrigerator until needed.

Thinly slice the reserved piece of cucumber with a mandoline or knife. Season with salt and plenty of white pepper.

Ladle the cucumber broth into serving bowls. Drain any liquid from the sliced cucumbers, then distribute them evenly among the bowls. Place a scoop of the crème fraîche–cucumber mixture on one tablespoon and use another to shape it into a neat, rounded shape (or quenelle). Place in the center of one bowl and repeat for the remaining bowls. Serve immediately.

Tips

The soup is lovely and simple on its own, but it also works well with ribbons of Parma or Serrano ham, cooked and shelled prawns, crawfish tails, or cooked crabmeat.

Keep the cucumber and celery in the refrigerator before making the soup; it will help the soup chill more quickly.

SUN'S OUT IN STOCKHOLM

LOVE THE TYPOGRAPHY ON THIS BUTCHER'S SIGN

OLD TOWN IN WARSAW

RADIS 'GLAÇONS' - ICE RADISHES AT THE MARKET IN PARIS

ON THE PLANE AGAIN FOR ANOTHER ADVENTURE.

CAFÉS IN KARAKÖY, ISTANBUL

FISH DOESN'T GET FRESHER THAN IN MARSEILLE.

MY KIND OF BREAKFAST: OYSTERS AND PINK PRAWNS IN BORDEAUX

JUICE SHOP IN ISTANBUL

lavender

oregano

wild thyme

STOCKHOLM - VENICE OF THE NORTH

Smörgåstårta

The Swedes might not be known for their extravagant design, opting more for snow-white interiors and simple lines, but when it comes to the humble sandwich, they certainly know how to push the boat out. *Smörgåstårta* is a sandwich layer-cake, filled with pâté, smoked fish, prawns, ham, cream cheese ... basically, anything. These sandwiches can be found in bakeries, supermarkets, and even at the petrol station, and are served at parties, weddings, funerals, and other social gatherings.

I went with the less-is-more approach for my filling, sticking with some key Swedish flavors: pickled beets, dill, quick-brined salmon, and horseradish.

For the quick-cured juniper salmon

1 cup water

2 tbsp coarse salt

2 tbsp granulated sugar

1 tsp juniper berries

1 small raw beet

5¼ oz very fresh salmon fillet, skinned

For the horseradish cream

6 tbsp heavy cream

1 tbsp prepared horseradish

4 slices Swedish flatbread (*polarbröd*) or good-quality sliced white bread, crusts removed

1 small cucumber

1 small pickled beet

1 unwaxed lemon

a few sprigs of dill

2 tbsp salmon roe

To make the quick-cured juniper salmon: Combine the water, salt, sugar, and juniper berries in a saucepan. Peel and coarsely chop the beet and add it to the pan. Bring to a boil, simmer to dissolve the sugar and salt, turn off the heat, and let cool to room temperature. Place in the refrigerator to chill.

Cut the salmon into thin slices. Drop them into the cold brine for 7 minutes, then remove, drain, and pat dry with a paper towel. Discard the brine.

To make the horseradish cream: Whisk the cream to firm-ish peaks, then fold in the horseradish.

Thinly spread each slice of bread with some of the horseradish cream and add a layer of salmon (reserve a few slices for garnish), then place the slices of bread on top of each other.

Using a peeler, peel thin ribbons from one side of the cucumber. Discard the first ribbon and don't use the seeded part; you need four perfect ribbons to wrap around the sandwich. With a melon baller, scoop enough balls of cucumber from the other sides of the cucumber, discarding the middle seeded part, to go around the edge of the bread.

Using a small offset spatula, spread the rest of the horseradish cream around the outside edges and top of the bread (like icing a cake), making sure the cream is nice and smooth. Delicately place the cucumber ribbons around the edges of the sandwich.

Use a mandoline to slice thin rounds of the pickled beet and very fine slices of the lemon. Decorate the top of your sandwich with the beet, lemon, dill, and cucumber balls. I like to put the cucumber balls around the top edge of the sandwich, and twist the remaining pieces of salmon around one finger to make rose shapes. Dot the salmon roe around. Chill until ready to serve.

Beef short ribs with crunchy slaw

Slow-roasted pork belly with sloe gin

Mains

-mustard glaze

"... every time a child says, 'I don't believe in fairies,' there is a fairy somewhere that falls down dead," Peter replies.

That's how I feel every time a journalist asks me what my favorite dish is. Okay, maybe comparing an interview question to the death of fairies is a little dramatic, but I do want to sigh every time I'm asked this. How can you ask someone who loves food what their favorite dish is? It's like asking Carrie from *Sex and the City* what her favorite pair of shoes is; it's impossible to answer. What I fancy eating depends on (a) what the weather is like, (b) where I am, and (c) the state of my refrigerator.

The recipes I've crammed into this chapter are the result of various different cravings or scenarios. On a hot summer's day, try my chicken summer salad (see page 126). When you need a quick dinner but have hardly anything in the refrigerator, my Zucchini Linguine with Three Different Sauces (page 136) is perfect. When you'd like to impress the in-laws, there's my Venison Steak with Celeriac Purée, Pickled Blackberries, and Carrot Petals (page 112). If you're entertaining a bunch of mates, my Seafood Chili with Tortilla Bowls (page 94). For a veggie, low-carb dinner, try my Stir-Fried Cauliflower Rice (page 121). For a simple, everyday dinner for the family, there's my Provençal Roast Chicken with Roasted Fennel (page 105). For a comforting TV dinner to kick back with, my Peeping Mushroom Pasta (page 79) is ideal.

Another question I'm often asked is what to cook for a romantic meal. My answer: Don't. Well, not on your first date, or your second, and possibly not even on your third. Nerves are not what you need when you're slaving over a meal and trying to look your best. Trust me. Having worked in professional kitchens, I know. However, if you're beyond the initial awkward dating stage, then (a) do your homework and ask your date what he or she does or doesn't like (I learned this lesson the hard way after serving meat to a vegetarian), (b) keep it simple, and (c) don't serve too much food (as this will make you sleepy ... you get my drift). A few dishes to help you with your romantic encounters are speedy Summer Spaghetti Bolognese (page 135), One-Pan Roast (page 76), or Mushroom Stroganoff with Spinach and Wild Rice (page 124).

Whatever your appetite, there's a recipe sure to satisfy it.

London loaf three ways

Serves	Preparation time:	Resting time:	Cooking time:
2 as a main course or 4 to 6 as a starter	20 minutes	15 minutes minimum	25 minutes

The London loaf. What is it? For me it used to be a standard white sandwich loaf. But with so many different national cuisines found across London, the true bread of the city goes far beyond the "London bloomer." From the sourdough loaves crafted under archways in east London to the Turkish *lahmacun* of Dalston and the naans of Brick Lane, there is no one bread that represents the city, but more a melting pot of doughs, revealing the diversity of the London food scene.

Flatbreads are the speediest of breads to make at home, and benefit the most from being freshly made to order. Here are three great ways to transform this simple dough into delicious pizzas.

For the beef topping (enough for 2 flatbreads)

3½ oz ground beef

5 cherry tomatoes, chopped

3 sage leaves, finely chopped

½ red onion, peeled and finely chopped

½ tsp sea salt

½ tsp white pepper

For the cheesy filling (enough for 2 flatbreads)

2 cloves of garlic, peeled

3 sprigs of lemon thyme

one 4½-oz ball buffalo mozzarella cheese

sea salt and freshly ground black pepper

a handful of fresh arugula

For the sweet topping (enough for 2 flatbreads)

heaping 2 tbsp mascarpone cheese

zest of 1 unwaxed lemon

1 tbsp maple syrup or runny honey

1 ripe peach or nectarine

To make the beef topping: Mix together all the ingredients in a bowl and set aside until needed.

To make the cheesy filling: Thinly slice the garlic, pick the leaves from the thyme, and tear the mozzarella roughly. Mix the garlic, thyme leaves, and mozzarella in a small bowl with some salt and black pepper. Set aside with the arugula.

To make the sweet topping: Mix the mascarpone with the lemon zest and maple syrup in a small bowl. Cut the peach in half, remove the pit, and thinly slice. Set aside.

To make the basic dough: Mix together the flour, baking powder, and salt in a large bowl. Make a well in the center and pour in the liquid ingredients. Combine until you have a slightly sticky mixture. Turn out onto a lightly floured surface and knead for a good 5 minutes, until you have a smooth ball. Transfer to a clean bowl and let rest for 15 minutes, covered with plastic wrap or a clean, damp kitchen towel.

Divide the dough into six balls. Lightly dust the work surface and use a rolling pin to roll out the dough balls into 6-in circles ⅛ to ¼ in thick.

Put a large nonstick frying pan over a high heat (do two pans at a time if you have them). Preheat the broiler.

For the beef flatbreads, put a dough round in the frying pan. Press half the beef mixture evenly on top and cook for 2 minutes, or until the base is golden and crisp. Place the flatbread under the broiler for 2 to 3 minutes, or until the meat is cooked. Repeat with another dough round and the remaining beef topping.

For cheesy flatbreads, put half the cheesy filling in the center of a dough round, along with half the arugula, leaving a margin around

For the basic dough
(makes 6 flatbreads)

2 cups all-purpose flour

1 tsp baking powder

1 tsp sea salt

7 tbsp plus 1 tsp warm water

¼ cup natural yogurt

1 tbsp vegetable oil

the edge. Fold the dough over to make a half-moon shape and press the edges to seal tightly. Place in the hot pan. Cook for 2 to 3 minutes on each side, or until golden. Repeat with another dough round and the remaining filling and arugula.

For sweet flatbreads, cook each dough round on one side for 2 minutes, then flip it over and cook the other side for another 2 minutes. Remove from the pan and spread the sweet topping on one side, then arrange the peach on top.

Serve the flatbreads immediately.

Tips

After you have rolled out the dough, work quite quickly, as it can dry out. Alternatively, cover with a loose layer of plastic wrap.

Be sure to heat the frying pan well before placing the dough in it.

Get ahead

The dough can be made the day before, wrapped, and stored in the refrigerator. (It's even better when made one day ahead.)

STEP BACK IN TIME
AT THIS ART SHOP.

LOVE THE VIEW FROM THE
FRONT SEATS ON A
LONDON DOUBLE DECKER

CLASSIC PIE 'N MASH SHOP,
EAST LONDON

CATCHING SOME SUN RAYS
ON DALSTON ROOF TOP

RAINY SUNDAY ACTIVITY:
SORTING OUT PHOTOS!

DELICIOUS SMELLS WAFTING
AROUND BRIXTON MARKET

BRITISH RED POST BOXES
ARE THE BEST!

A LITTLE BIT OF PINK
AND A FULL MOON

DON'T SEE MANY OF THESE
AROUND TOWN ANYMORE.

55 SHOREDITCH

LONDON

TELEPHONE

BLACKHORSE ROAD

TOTTENHAM HALE

WALTHAMSTOW CENTRAL

SEVEN SISTERS

VICTORIA LINE

FINSBURY PARK

EUSTON

KING'S CROSS-ST PANCRAS

HIGHBURY & ISLINGTON

OXFORD CIRCUS

WARREN STREET

GREEN PARK

VICTORIA

PIMLICO

VAUXHALL

STOCKWELL

BRIXTON

UNDERGROUND

Potato crumpets with maple-mustard glaze

Serves	Preparation time:	Resting time:	Cooking time:
4	30 minutes	1 to 2 hours	40 minutes

Back when I was a kid, breakfast for dinner was far more de rigueur, whether it was a sneaky fry-up, beans on toast, or kippers. This is a fancy version of a fry-up. Here the pillowy potato crumpets stand in for the more traditional heavy hash browns, while the blistered tomatoes are a speedy and fresh substitute for ketchup.

½ cup plus 3 tbsp milk

7 tbsp water

1¼ cups potato flour

½ cup plus 2 tbsp all-purpose flour

¼ tsp fast-acting yeast

9 oz cherry tomatoes on the vine

sea salt

½ tsp baking powder

4 to 6 tbsp sunflower or vegetable oil

2 large cured ham steaks

2 tsp brown mustard

2 tsp maple syrup

4 eggs

Warm the milk and water gently in a small saucepan. Put both flours and the yeast into a bowl and mix well. Add the milk and water and whisk until smooth. It will be the consistency of heavy cream. Cover with plastic wrap and let rest at room temperature for 1 to 2 hours, or until bubbles have formed on the surface.

Preheat the oven to 400°F. Put the tomatoes on a parchment paper–lined baking sheet, sprinkle with salt, and place in the oven for 10 minutes, or until the tomatoes have burst. Set aside and turn the oven temperature to 325°F.

Whisk ½ tsp salt and the baking powder into the batter. Put a heavy frying pan over medium-high heat and pour in 2 tbsp of the oil. Grease a 3½-in pastry ring, place it in the pan, and pour ⅓ cup of batter into it. Turn the heat to medium-low and cook for 5 minutes or so, or until the surface has just set and bubbles have formed. Remove the ring and flip the crumpet over. Cook for 2 to 3 minutes, or until golden on the other side.

Repeat with the remaining batter; this should make 5 crumpets in total. Set aside on a wire rack.

Put 1 tbsp oil in a large frying pan and heat until medium-hot. Add the ham steaks and cook for 1 to 2 minutes on one side. Flip them over and fry for 1 minute longer. Spread the tops with the mustard, then the maple syrup, and slide out of the pan. Use a 3¼-in cookie cutter to cut out 4 pieces from the ham steaks. Keep warm on a baking sheet in the oven while you make the eggs.

Grease four 3½-in pastry rings. Put 1 tbsp oil in the pan, crack the eggs into the rings, and fry the eggs for 2 to 3 minutes, or until the whites have set. Divide the potato crumpets among four plates. Put a ham slice and fried egg on top of each one, and drape the vine tomatoes over them before serving.

Bread-wrapped lamb kebabs

Serves
2 to 4

Preparation time:
20 minutes

Cooking time:
15 minutes

Istanbul really is the capital of street food, but not of the greasy fast-food variety. On every street corner you can spot people grilling fish, meat, and vegetables; the smells waft through the air, luring you.

A tasty mix of grilled meat wrapped in flatbread to soak up the flavorsome juices, some fresh grilled peppers, and a soothing yogurt and pomegranate sauce on the side is what a truly tasty Turkish kebab is about.

For the super-speedy flatbread

scant 1½ cups unbleached bread flour

1 tsp sea salt

6 tbsp hot water

For the vegetable skewers

3 red onions

4 small green bell peppers

For the lamb kebabs

3½ oz mix of lamb kidneys and liver

7 oz ground lamb

½ tsp red pepper flakes

1 tsp sea salt

½ tsp sumac

1 tbsp fresh thyme leaves

olive oil

runny yogurt

1 tbsp pomegranate molasses

sea salt and freshly ground pepper

1 head iceberg lettuce, cut into wedges

If using wooden skewers, soak them in water for 30 minutes.

To make the flatbread: Put the flour and salt in a large bowl. Pour in the hot water and knead for 2 to 3 minutes, until you have a smooth ball of dough. Cover with a clean, damp kitchen towel (don't skip this, as the dough will dry out) and set aside.

To make the vegetable skewers: Peel and quarter the onions, keeping the stems intact. Cut the bell peppers into thirds horizontally. Thread the vegetables onto four skewers, alternating the colors.

To make the lamb kebabs: Very finely chop the kidneys and liver. Mix together with the ground lamb, red pepper flakes, salt, sumac, and thyme leaves and massage together to combine. Divide the meat into four portions and squeeze it onto the ends of four skewers, covering about 4 in. Set aside.

Preheat the broiler to high. Divide the dough into four pieces. On a floured surface, roll each one out into a rectangle, rolling as thinly as you can (use the size of the meat part of your kebab as a guide, as you want it to wrap around the kebab, covering the meat).

Rub the lamb kebabs with a little oil. Broil for 1 minute on each side, then remove from the heat. Wrap the flatbread around the skewer until the meat is just covered, then trim away and discard the excess dough. Seal the overlap with a dab of water, squeeze the ends of the kebab together lightly, and place on a parchment paper–lined baking sheet. Repeat with the remaining kebabs. Place under the broiler, turning regularly for about 7 minutes, or until the dough is golden and cooked thoroughly.

Rub the vegetable skewers with a little oil and heat a griddle pan or the broiler. Cook for about 5 minutes, or until charred on each side.

Place the yogurt in a bowl, swirl the pomegranate molasses through, and season with salt and pepper. Serve with the lamb kebabs, vegetable skewers, and wedges of iceberg.

Swiss chard is a common fixture on menus in the Nice region of France. But, oddly, it's more popular in pastry shops and bakeries than anywhere else, where it fills the famous tourte de blette, a sweet pastry that is also filled with raisins, pine nuts, and sometimes pastry cream. It's quite an acquired taste, to say the least. I even spotted chard ice cream in Nice's most famous ice-cream parlor, Fenocchio, which offers some other unusual flavors too, such as black olive and sun-dried tomato.

Confit cod with rainbow chard gratin

Serves
4

Preparation time:
20 minutes

Cooking time:
30 minutes

For the chard gratin

1 cup rainbow chard, stalks cut into 1-in pieces and leaves cut into wide ribbons

1 cup crème fraîche

2 egg yolks

3½ oz Parmesan cheese, finely grated

sea salt and freshly ground pepper

2 tbsp olive oil

2 large slices sourdough bread, torn into large pieces

For the cod

4 cloves of garlic

3 cups olive oil

zest of 1 unwaxed lemon

4 sprigs of thyme

four 5-oz cod fillets (thick, middle piece of cod), skinned and deboned; remove from refrigerator 30 minutes before cooking

sea salt and freshly ground pepper

For the persillade

2 cloves of garlic, peeled and minced

small handful of finely chopped fresh flat-leaf parsley leaves

3 tbsp extra-virgin olive oil

2 tsp white wine vinegar

sea salt and freshly ground pepper

While northern France is all about butter, head down south to Provence and olive oil is everywhere. Traditionally, to "confit" means to cook duck legs or other meat slowly in their own fat. My version makes the most of the local olive oil and is lightened with the use of white fish; the slow poaching keeps its delicate texture.

To make the chard gratin: Preheat the oven to 350°F.

Bring a large saucepan of water to a boil, add the chard stalks, and blanch for 5 minutes, adding the leaves for the final 2 minutes. Drain and cool in running water before setting aside to drain thoroughly.

In a bowl, mix the crème fraîche with the egg yolks and half the Parmesan cheese, then season with salt and pepper.

Place the drained chard in an 8-by-8-in ovenproof dish. Pour the crème fraîche mixture over the top and sprinkle with the remaining cheese. Bake for 20 minutes.

Meanwhile, heat the oil in a frying pan, then stir in the bread. Cook the croutons for about 4 minutes, stirring often, until a nice deep golden brown. Set aside until ready to serve.

To make the cod: Put the garlic in a large sauté pan with the oil. Add the lemon zest, along with the thyme sprigs. Gently heat the oil until bubbles are coming off the garlic, but it isn't cooking quickly. You want it to have small bubbles but no sizzle.

Place the cod fillets in the pan and cook on the lowest heat for 5 to 8 minutes, depending on the thickness of the cod. You will notice the texture change to flaky and the color turn opaque when ready. Using a slotted spoon, remove the cod from the oil. Season with salt and pepper and set on a cooling rack to drain.

To make the persillade: Mix the garlic, parsley, oil, and vinegar in a small bowl, then season with salt and pepper.

Remove the chard gratin from the oven and sprinkle the crispy croutons over the top. Serve the cod with the chard gratin and a spoonful of persillade on top.

One—tray roast

Serves 4

Preparation time: 20 minutes

Cooking time: 1 hour 40 minutes

My interest in roasting quail stemmed from the limitations of my little-Paris-kitchen oven. Chickens and turkeys are tricky to cook at the best of times, even in large kitchens. Ideally they are brined the day before, roasted while all the vegetables are also in the oven, and presented on an impressive platter at the table. But my little Paris kitchen was no place for such endeavors. So I learned to adapt a traditional roast for pocket-size feasts. Quails are dinky and delicious, and fit snugly in a small roasting pan, the only kind that would fit in my shoebox-size oven.

four 7-oz oven-ready quails

sea salt and freshly ground pepper

1 unwaxed lemon

1⅓ cups light-colored beer

7 tbsp runny honey

⅓ cup fresh flat-leaf parsley leaves

10 oz pork sausages

8 carrots, peeled and halved lengthwise

12 oz new potatoes, washed and halved

heaping 1 tbsp whole-grain mustard

7 tbsp heavy cream

Preheat the oven to 400°F.

Season the quails with plenty of salt and pepper. Zest the lemon and rub into the quail skins with the seasoning.

Juice the lemon, keeping the juiced halves. Mix the beer with the honey and lemon juice and set aside.

Finely chop the parsley and the juiced lemon skins, removing the seeds. Remove and discard the casing from the sausages and mix the sausage meat with the parsley, lemon, and some salt and pepper.

Stuff the quail cavities with the sausage mix. There is a generous amount and it needs to be pushed in to fit. Take four long pieces of kitchen twine and truss each quail around the legs to close the filled cavity. Place the quails breast-side down in a roasting pan with the carrots and potatoes.

Pour over the beer marinade and cover with aluminum foil. Roast for 1 hour. Remove the foil, reserving it for later, and turn over each quail so that they're breast-side up. Roast, uncovered, for another 25 minutes, or until the quail are golden and the juices run clear when the meat is pierced with a sharp knife.

Drain all the roasting pan juices into a large frying pan. Set the quail and vegetables aside, covered with the foil. Bring the cooking juices to a boil and cook for 7 to 8 minutes, or until reduced by half. Stir in the mustard and cream and taste for seasoning.

Divide the carrots, potatoes, and quail among four plates. Pour the creamy sauce over and serve immediately.

Tip
Other ground meat may be substituted for the pork sausage.

Peeping mushroom pasta

Serves
4

Preparation time:
30 minutes

Cooking time:
40 minutes

Creamy sauce and earthy mushrooms is a tried and tested combination that never fails. Many might think it's a little boring and old school, but I've discovered a fun way of pepping up a classic. Replace boring button mushrooms with some exotic Asian mushrooms and the recipe gets an instant facelift; pair them with lots of bubbling cheese and you are onto a winner.

2 tbsp butter

¼ cup all-purpose flour

2 cups lukewarm milk, plus more as needed

¼ onion, peeled

1 whole clove

1 bay leaf

9 oz rigatoni pasta

pinch of freshly ground nutmeg

sea salt and white pepper

2 tbsp whole-grain mustard

3½ oz Gruyère, Parmesan, or other hard cheese, grated

6 oz mixed enoki or shimeji mushrooms, trimmed and torn into single mushrooms

finely chopped fresh parsley for serving

Melt the butter in a medium frying pan over medium heat. Add the flour and mix to form a paste, cooking it for 2 minutes. Remove from the heat and let cool for 2 minutes, then gradually add the milk, whisking continuously.

Place the pan back over medium heat; add the onion, clove, and bay leaf; and simmer gently for 10 minutes, whisking frequently. If the sauce becomes too thick, whisk in a little more milk 1 tbsp at a time until saucy.

Preheat the oven to 350°F.

Bring a stockpot of salted water to a boil. Put the pasta in the water and cook for 2 minutes less than the package instructions say.

Finish the sauce by removing the onion, clove, and bay leaf, then adding the nutmeg and seasoning with salt and white pepper. Stir in the mustard and half the cheese.

Drain the pasta and arrange the rigatoni pieces upright tightly in four ovenproof dishes; they will look a bit like honeycomb. Pour the sauce over the pasta. Tap the base of the baking dishes to allow the sauce to get between the holes, spooning more on if necessary. Place the mushroom stalks into the rigatoni holes, leaving the caps poking out. Sprinkle with the remaining cheese.

Bake for 20 to 25 minutes, or until the cheese is golden and bubbling. Serve with a sprinkle of finely chopped parsley on top.

Get ahead

Make up the pasta dishes a few hours before, but add 10 minutes to the cooking time if baking straight from the refrigerator.

The sauce (béchamel) can be made up to 1 day in advance. Place some plastic wrap directly on the sauce when storing in the refrigerator to prevent a skin from forming. Whisk well to break up any lumps before using.

Salt beef with horseradish mash

Serves 4 to 6	Preparation time: 45 minutes	Curing time: 3 to 10 days	Cooking time: 3 to 4 hours

For the brine

7 tbsp light brown muscovado sugar

1¼ cups coarse sea salt

1 tsp peppercorns

4 juniper berries, lightly bruised

2 star anise

4 whole cloves

3 bay leaves

6½ cups water

One 2½-lb beef brisket

1 onion, halved

1 carrot

1 stalk celery

1 bay leaf

5 peppercorns

For the dill vinaigrette

2 tbsp fresh dill

¼ cup sunflower oil

¼ cup white wine vinegar

1 tsp sea salt

large pinch of sugar

For the mash

2½ lb russet potatoes

2 knobs of butter

½ to ¾ cup milk, warmed

1 tbsp prepared horseradish

sea salt

mustard and cornichons or sliced gherkins for serving

Brisket is a fatty and great-value cut from the front underside of the cow. It is most commonly used to make pastrami and corned beef, which has seen quite a comeback in recent years. For many, however, it has always been on the map, particularly for fans like myself who make a regular pilgrimage to Beigel Bake on Brick Lane for their exemplary salt beef bagels with lashings of English mustard.

To make the brine: Place all the ingredients in a large saucepan. Bring to a boil and simmer for 5 minutes, stirring to dissolve the salt and sugar. Leave to cool completely.

Place the beef in a lidded plastic container and pour the brine over the top. Make sure it is fully submerged (you may have to weigh it down with something) and place in the refrigerator for a minimum of 3 days, or up to 10 days. Turn the meat daily.

When ready to cook, drain the beef, discarding the brine, and rinse under cold running water. Place in a large saucepan and cover with cold water. Add the onion, carrot, celery, bay leaf, and peppercorns. Gently bring to a simmer, skimming off any scum that comes to the surface. Poach gently, uncovered, for 3 to 4 hours, topping with just-boiled water if necessary.

To make the dill vinaigrette: Blend the dill (stalks included) in a food processor or blender with the other ingredients.

To make the mash: Peel the potatoes and boil them in salted water for 20 to 25 minutes, or until tender. Drain and put back into the pan over medium heat, stirring continuously, until dry. Once the potatoes have stopped steaming, mash them or pass through a potato ricer. Mix with the butter and add enough warm milk to make a smooth, creamy mash. Add the horseradish and season with salt.

When the beef is ready, remove it from the pan and place on a cutting board, then thinly slice it. Serve the beef, warm or hot, with the mash on the side and mustard and plenty of cornichons. Drizzle with the dill vinaigrette.

Get ahead
The beef freezes well once cooked. The vinaigrette can be made a day in advance.

Slow-roasted pork belly with sloe gin

Serves	Preparation time:	Marinating time:	Cooking time:
4 to 6	30 minutes	4 hours or overnight	3½ to 4 hours

Slow-cooked pork belly has to be one of the most tender cuts, thanks to the rich layers of fat that sandwich the flesh. I like to offset the fattiness of the meat with something fresh and crunchy, which is where the iceberg wedge comes into play. Try this dish as a lighter and more summery take on the traditional roast belly of pork.

½ cup plus 2 tbsp sloe gin

6 tbsp runny honey

2 tsp white pepper

1 tbsp red wine vinegar

one 2-lb boneless pork belly, skin scored and patted dry

1 tbsp sea salt flakes

4 red onions, peeled and quartered

7 oz red currants or mixed berries (frozen is fine), plus a handful to garnish

1 head iceberg lettuce

1 unwaxed lemon

scant 1 cup thick Greek yogurt

pinch of granulated sugar

pinch of sea salt

Mix the sloe gin, honey, white pepper, and vinegar in a shallow glass or ceramic dish. Place the pork in it carefully, making sure that the marinade doesn't touch the skin. Leave uncovered and place in the refrigerator for 4 hours, or as long as 2 days.

Preheat the oven to 425°F.

Pat the skin of the pork dry with a paper towel. Place on a tray, setting the marinade to one side, and use a blow-dryer for 2 to 3 minutes to remove all the excess moisture from the skin. Rub the skin thoroughly with the salt flakes, getting into the scoring.

Place the red onions and currants at the bottom of a roasting pan, then pour over the marinade and lay the pork belly skin-side up on top. Roast for 30 minutes, then turn the oven temperature to 300°F and roast for 2½ to 3 hours, or until very tender.

Remove the pork from the oven. Take out the onions and currants and set aside. Crank the heat to 425°F and place the pork back in the oven for about 10 minutes, or until the skin is crispy.

Remove the pork from the oven. When cool enough to handle, separate the skin from the flesh. Slice the pork belly into slivers and chop the skin into small crouton-size pieces. Cut the lettuce into thick slices, then wash and dry (keeping them whole).

Finely zest the lemon and mix into the Greek yogurt with the sugar and sea salt. Add a squeeze of lemon juice.

Place a large wedge of iceberg on a plate and top with the pork, onions, skin, and currants. Drizzle with the yogurt dressing.

Tip

If you can't get ahold of sloe gin, use cassis or a light fruity red wine like Grenache.

Seafood paella nests

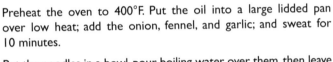

Serves
6

Preparation time:
25 minutes

Cooking time:
1 hour

The traditional rice-based paella has traveled far beyond its Valencian birthplace; I see giant paella pans bubbling away at my local market on a Saturday. But when I visited Toc al Mar, a quiet nook along the Spanish coast, I discovered a delicious, little-known variation known as *fiduea*, made with vermicelli noodles. Inspired by this discovery, I decided to make my own version, but my paella nests are too tantalizing a secret not to share.

2 tbsp olive oil

1 medium onion, peeled, halved and finely sliced

1 small bulb of fennel, trimmed and finely sliced

2 cloves of garlic, peeled and sliced

5 oz rice vermicelli noodles

2 knobs of soft butter

1 chorizo sausage, cut into thin rounds

10 tbsp dry white wine

generous pinch of saffron

3 cups fish stock

8½ oz unshelled raw king prawns

7 oz cod or monkfish cheeks

5 oz purple sprouting broccoli, stalks and florets separated and roughly chopped, tough stalks discarded

1¼ lb mixed clams and mussels, cleaned

Preheat the oven to 400°F. Put the oil into a large lidded pan over low heat; add the onion, fennel, and garlic; and sweat for 10 minutes.

Put the noodles in a bowl, pour boiling water over them, then leave for about 20 seconds, or until they are pliable but still have bite. Drain and spread out on a clean kitchen towel to get rid of excess moisture. Pat dry with another kitchen towel until the noodles are very dry. Brush the wells of a muffin pan with the butter and line the wells with the noodles. Make sure you push the noodles right to the top of the wells, as they will shrink slightly. Bake for 20 to 25 minutes, or until crisp and golden.

Add the chorizo to the onion mixture and fry, uncovered, for 8 to 10 minutes, or until golden. Add the white wine and saffron and simmer for 1 minute, then add the stock. Bring to a boil. Add the prawns, fish cheeks, and broccoli stalks to the pan and stir. Simmer for 1 minute, then add the clams, mussels, and broccoli florets. Toss to coat with the sauce, cover with the lid, crank the heat to high, and cook for 3 minutes.

Strain the stew through a colander over a large bowl. Return the liquid to the pan and simmer for about 20 minutes, or until reduced to your desired consistency (either a broth or a rich sauce).

Meanwhile, remove some of the mussels and clams from their shells and add the meat to the fish-broccoli mixture, then cover with aluminum foil to keep warm.

Remove the vermicelli nests from the oven and divide among large shallow bowls. Add a ladleful of the seafood and broccoli to each of the nests, then pour the sauce over the top. Arrange more of the seafood and broccoli around the edge of the nests to serve.

Get ahead
The nests can be made in advance and kept in an airtight container for a day or two.

Spice—rubbed trout with giant couscous and green beans

Serves
4

Preparation time:
30 minutes

Cooking time:
20 minutes

When it comes to spice rubs, I have some friends who guard their personal recipe the same way Coca-Cola guards theirs. I am, however, happy to share my special blend of spices. Making your own custom spice rub is probably the simplest way of adding your own personal touch to dishes. This recipe is really just a starting point and can be easily adapted to your taste. Once you get the hang of balancing the flavors, the possibilities are endless.

For the spice rub

2 tbsp sumac

1 tbsp smoked paprika

1 tbsp granulated sugar

1 tbsp sea salt

1 tbsp ground cumin

½ tbsp ground ginger

½ tbsp ground cinnamon

4 whole trout (about 10½ oz each), gutted and scaled

1½ unwaxed lemons

1 small bulb of fennel, halved and finely sliced, keeping the leafy tops

large handful of flat-leaf parsley leaves, coarsely chopped

1½ cups Israeli couscous

8½ oz French green beans, cut into ¼-in pieces

1 tbsp olive oil

sea salt

Preheat the broiler to high. Line a baking sheet with aluminum foil and lightly oil the foil.

To make the spice rub: Blend all the ingredients with a pestle and mortar.

Smear the spice rub generously all over the outside and inside of the trout, then place on the prepared baking sheet

Thinly slice the whole lemon. Stuff the fennel, parsley, and lemon slices inside the cavities of the fish. Broil the fish for 5 to 10 minutes on one side, then turn the fish and cook for another 5 minutes on the other side.

Meanwhile, bring a pot of salted water to a boil and add the couscous. Boil for 3 minutes, then add the green beans. Cook for 2 minutes, or until al dente, and drain.

Zest and juice the remaining lemon half. Toss the couscous and beans with the oil, lemon zest, lemon juice, and salt. Serve each fish whole with the couscous on the side. Garnish with the fennel tops.

Tip

This spice rub works well with all sorts of other things. Try spreading it on eggplant slices and drizzling with a little oil before grilling. It's also a great rub for chicken.

Get ahead

Make the spice rub a few days before and keep in a sealed jar. You can easily double the quantity and store it to season other dishes.

Beef short ribs with crunchy slaw

Serves 4	Preparation time: 20 minutes	Marinating time: 1 hour to 2 days	Cooking time: 2½ to 3½ hours

I have a fond memory of my Austrian grandma eating ribs with a big bib stuck into the collar of her dress. I think the best way of eating ribs is with your fingers. This is definitely finger food—not in the dainty, ladylike sense, but more in the messy kind of way.

For the marinade

one 15-oz can cherry tomatoes

¼ cup firmly packed dark brown sugar

1 tbsp tomato purée

1 dried chipotle chile, finely chopped

2 tsp white pepper

6 tbsp red wine vinegar

1 tbsp fish sauce or Worcestershire sauce

5 cloves of garlic, peeled and minced

3 to 4½ lb beef short ribs

For the slaw

8½ oz celeriac

4 carrots

1 crunchy red dessert apple

½ cup plus 2 tbsp crème fraîche

¼ cup white wine vinegar

1 tbsp whole-grain mustard

pinch of sugar

sea salt and freshly ground black pepper

2 green onions, finely chopped

To make the marinade: Put all the ingredients into a bowl and mix well.

Place the ribs and the marinade in a large resealable bag to marinate for at least 1 hour, or up to 2 days (ribs are best when marinated several hours or longer).

Preheat the oven to 300°F. Transfer the ribs and the marinade from the bag to a large baking pan. Cover with aluminum foil and roast for 2 to 3 hours, or until the meat is tender and beginning to fall apart. Increase the oven temperature to 400°F. Remove the foil and baste the ribs with the marinade. Roast for 30 minutes longer, basting a couple of times. The sauce should be sticky and thick and the ribs dark and glossy.

Remove from the oven and let cool until you can pick the ribs up with your fingers. If you want to thicken the sauce further, remove the ribs, cover them with foil, and set aside. Place the sauce in a small saucepan and simmer until it's the desired consistency, then brush over the ribs before serving.

In the meantime, to make the slaw: Peel; then, using a mandoline or food processor, cut the celeriac and carrots into fine little matchsticks, or grate them. Peel and core the apple, then cut into matchsticks, or grate. Put the celeriac, carrots, and apple into a bowl. Whisk together the rest of the slaw ingredients and toss through the salad. Taste for seasoning.

Line up the ribs and sprinkle the green onions down the middle. Serve with the slaw on the side.

Tip

Using a mandoline to julienne your vegetables really makes a difference. The slaw will have a crunchier texture (grating it will make the slaw wetter).

Get ahead

You can marinate the ribs up to 2 days in advance.

Make sure you prepare the slaw at the last moment; the celeriac and apple will turn brown otherwise.

Pasta pizza bianca e rossa

Serves 4 to 6	Preparation time: 15 minutes	Cooking time: 30 minutes

I nipped into quite a few bakeries while visiting Naples, and kept spotting *frittatine di pasta*—deep-fried pasta balls, stuffed with peas, ground pork, and béchamel sauce; the recipe was born from using up leftover pasta. When you can't decide whether you want pizza or pasta, have a pasta pizza.

For the sauce

one 15-oz can cherry tomatoes

1 tsp dried oregano

good pinch of granulated sugar

pinch of sea salt

For the pasta base

10½ oz dried spaghetti

4 eggs

pinch of dried oregano

½ tsp sea salt

½ tsp freshly ground pepper

2 tbsp olive oil

For the bianca

4½ oz soft goat's cheese

6 slices Parma ham

Olive oil for drizzling

½ tsp red pepper flakes (optional)

For the rossa

¼ cup pitted black olives

6 anchovy fillets, drained

6 large fresh basil leaves

To make the sauce: Put the tomatoes and oregano into a medium saucepan with the sugar and salt and bring to a simmer. Cook for 5 minutes, then blend with an immersion blender until smooth. Taste and adjust the seasonings if necessary. Turn the heat to low and keep warm.

To make the pasta base: Bring a stockpot of salted water to a boil. Add the spaghetti and cook for about 10 minutes, or until al dente, then drain. Tip the pasta onto a clean kitchen towel and roll the pasta in the towel to remove all excess moisture.

In a large bowl, beat the eggs with the oregano, salt, and pepper. Place the pasta in the bowl with the eggs and toss with your hands to coat thoroughly.

Preheat the broiler to high. Put a large ovenproof frying pan over medium heat and pour in 1 tbsp of the oil. When the oil in the pan is really hot, add half the pasta and spread out evenly across the surface of the pan. Fry for 4 minutes, or until the base is really golden and crunchy. Repeat with the remaining pasta to make a second pasta pizza base.

To make the bianca: Scatter half the goat's cheese in even lumps over the top of one pizza base. Place under the broiler for 4 to 5 minutes. Tear the ham in ribbons, distribute half over the cheese, then drizzle with a little oil and sprinkle with the red pepper flakes (if using).

To make the rossa: Top the second pizza base with tomato sauce, along with the olives and anchovies. Place under the broiler for 4 to 5 minutes, then arrange the basil leaves over the top.

Serve immediately.

Tips

If you're using leftover pasta, you need cooked spaghetti.

Make sure the oil is nice and hot before the pasta goes in the pan.

Don't skip the drying stage of the pasta preparation or you will end up with a watery mixture.

Ham hock lunchbox

Serves
4 to 6

Preparation time:
20 minutes

Cooking time:
3½ to 4½ hours

I was the queen of packed lunches when I had an office job in London. My boss would often make fun of me, saying my packed lunch resembled a three-course meal. I certainly wasn't content with a soggy sandwich from a vending machine. Now I work mainly from home and a lunchbox isn't so important; however, I do like to head out to the park when the sun is shining, and this is a perfect portable lunch.

2 lightly smoked ham hocks (about 2½ lb each)

2 onions, peeled and halved

2 carrots, peeled and halved lengthwise

2 stalks celery, halved

2 bay leaves

1 tsp peppercorns

For the potato salad

1 lb baby new potatoes, scrubbed

½ cup crème fraîche

3 tbsp chopped chives

juice of ½ lemon

sea salt and freshly ground pepper

8½ oz sugar snap peas

2 tbsp olive oil

1 tbsp balsamic vinegar

sea salt and freshly ground pepper

Place the ham hocks in a large saucepan and cover with cold water, then bring to a boil. Boil for 2 to 3 minutes, then drain. Return the ham hocks to the pan and cover once more with cold water. Add the onions, carrots, celery, bay leaves, and peppercorns.

Bring to a boil over medium heat, skimming off any scum that rises to the surface. Lower the heat and simmer, uncovered, for 3 to 4 hours, or until the flesh on the ham hocks is tender enough to pull away from the bone. Top with just-boiled water to keep the hocks covered while cooking, if necessary. Drain the liquid and reserve for another use (it makes a great stock for the Speedy One-Pot Noodle on page 102). Set the hocks aside to cool before shedding.

To make the potato salad: Place the potatoes in a pan of cold, salted water, bring to a boil, and cook for 15 to 20 minutes, or until tender when pierced with a fork.

Mix the crème fraîche, chives, and lemon juice in a small bowl, then season with salt and pepper. Drain the potatoes well in a large colander and crush gently with the back of a fork (breaking them up allows the dressing to penetrate them better). Transfer the potatoes to a large bowl and fold in the crème fraîche dressing while they're still warm. Set aside to cool completely.

Cook the sugar snap peas in boiling, salted water for 1 minute, then drain and cool in a colander placed under running cold water. Transfer the sugar snap peas to a small bowl. Whisk the oil and balsamic vinegar with some salt and pepper. Pour over the sugar snap peas and toss to coat well.

Pack each dish in different sections of your lunchbox and store in the refrigerator for up to 1 day.

Seafood chili with tortilla bowls

Serves
8
(with some left over)

Preparation time:
30 minutes
(plus soaking time for
dried beans, if using)

Cooking time:
2 hours

I love spicy food. I try to sneak a bit of chile into almost everything I eat, from cheese on toast to a simple salad with a spicy dressing, or grilled fish with a good smear of chile paste. Inevitably my chilies end up rather spicy too, so I always serve them with a cool dollop of sour cream to offset the heat.

14 oz dried black beans or three 15-oz cans black beans, drained

1 tbsp vegetable oil, plus more for brushing

1 red onion, peeled and finely chopped

1 bunch green onions, chopped and separated into green and white parts

2 dried chipotle chiles

6 cloves of garlic, peeled and crushed

2 tbsp tomato purée

1 tsp ground cumin

pinch of ground cinnamon

1 tbsp paprika

two 15-oz cans cherry tomatoes

2 ears of corn or one 8.5-oz can corn, drained

6 plain flour tortillas

7 oz mixed smoked fish, such as haddock, salmon, and cod

7 oz mixed seafood, such as prawns, squid, and clams

For the sour cream sauce

¾ cup plus 2 tbsp sour cream

zest and juice of 1 lime

pinch of sea salt

pinch of granulated sugar

wedges of lime for serving

If using dried beans, soak them overnight in plenty of cold water. Drain and give them a rinse. Place in a large saucepan of cold water and bring to a boil. Skim off any scum that floats to the surface and simmer for 1 hour. Let them cool completely in the water, then drain.

Heat the oil in a large saucepan over a medium heat, then add the red onion, white parts of the green onions, chiles, and garlic. Fry for about 5 minutes, or until the onions are translucent and soft. Add the tomato purée, cumin, cinnamon, and paprika and cook for 2 minutes, then add the cherry tomatoes.

Fill both tomato cans with water and pour into the saucepan.

Stir in the cooked beans and simmer, uncovered, for 45 minutes. The sauce will reduce and thicken. (If using canned beans, stir them in during the last 5 minutes of cooking.) Taste for seasoning and discard the chipotle chiles.

Husk the corn. Cut the kernels off the cobs (see tip) and set aside.

Preheat the oven to 325°F. Place six ovenproof mugs or small bowls on a baking sheet. Brush one side of the tortillas with oil and press them tightly oil-side down into the mugs or bowls. Bake for 8 to 10 minutes, or until crisp and golden.

Five minutes before serving, heat a large ovenproof nonstick frying pan in the oven. When hot, brush with oil, add the fish, and cook for 2 minutes, shaking the pan after 1 minute to make sure the fish doesn't stick. Add the seafood and corn and cook for 3 to 4 minutes.

To make the sour cream sauce: Mix all the ingredients together and set aside.

Stir and taste the chili for seasoning. Place a tortilla bowl on each plate and ladle in the chili. Top with a dollop of sour cream sauce, a spoonful of seafood and corn, and sprinkle some of the green parts of the green onions over the top. Serve immediately (to avoid the bowls becoming soggy), with wedges of lime on the side.

Tips

Place the tortillas in the microwave or oven for a few seconds if they are not pliable enough to press into the mugs or bowls.

If you prefer the traditional ground meat, just add it to the pan with the onions. Make sure to brown it nicely and drain off any fat before adding the rest of the ingredients.

To remove corn kernels from the cob, put a glass bowl on a kitchen towel (to keep the bowl from slipping). Fold a piece of paper towel and place in the center of the bowl. Rest one end of the corn cob on the paper towel and use a sharp knife to cut off the corn kernels, catching them all in the bowl.

Get ahead

Bean chili is even better when made the day before (as the spices infuse the mix). Just fry the seafood and make the bowls before serving.

The sour cream sauce can also be made a day in advance.

Snap, crackle, and pop fish

Serves	Preparation time:	Cooking time:
4	20 minutes	35 minutes

Fish, chips, and mushy peas—a British gastronomic perennial. The paper wrap, the smell of malt vinegar, and the crisp, golden-battered fish.... Unfortunately, deep-frying at home is not as easy as it is at the chippie. I like to leave deep-frying to the professionals and avoid the havoc it can cause in the kitchen. A slick of grease down the hostess is particularly best avoided if you are cooking for guests.

I know what you are thinking; puffed rice might be an odd thing to use, but it works miraculously well, giving the fish a crisp, crunchy coating without the greasy aftertaste and the guilt of a batter-drenched piece of fish.

2½ lb waxy potatoes, scrubbed and well dried

¼ cup olive oil

sea salt

14 oz frozen peas

1 bunch of mint, leaves and stems separated

2 unwaxed lemons, zested and cut into wedges

heaping ½ cup thick Greek yogurt

freshly ground pepper

four 5-oz tail-end fillets cod or pollack, skinned and deboned

¼ cup all-purpose flour

1 egg, beaten

½ cup puffed rice cereal

2 tbsp canola oil

Tartar Sauce (page 249)

malt vinegar for serving (optional)

Preheat the oven to 425°F. Line a baking sheet with parchment paper.

Cut the potatoes lengthwise into ⅜-in-thick fries, leaving the skin on. Place the potatoes in a large pan of cold water. Bring the water to a boil, then cook for 1 minute before draining in a colander. The potatoes should still be uncooked and firm to the touch.

Put the potatoes on a large cutting board lined with a kitchen towel and blot them dry. The drier they are, the crispier they will be after cooking. Put the potatoes on the prepared baking sheet in one layer, mix with the olive oil, and season with salt. Roast for 35 minutes, turning the potatoes every 10 to 15 minutes.

Place the frozen peas, mint stems, lemon zest, and 2 tbsp water in a saucepan. Cover and cook for 5 minutes. Discard the mint stems.

Roughly chop the mint leaves and combine in a blender with the peas and yogurt. Blend until you have a chunky purée. Season with salt and pepper and add a squeeze of lemon juice. Transfer to a saucepan and keep warm over low heat until ready to serve.

Season the fish fillets with salt and pepper. Set up three shallow bowls, one with the flour, one with the beaten egg, and one with the puffed rice. Dip each piece of fish in the flour, then in the egg, then press firmly into the puffed rice to coat the fish well and evenly.

Put the canola oil in a large nonstick frying pan over medium heat. Add the fish fillets and fry on one side for 3 to 4 minutes, or until golden brown, then turn and fry for 3 to 4 minutes more.

Serve the fish with the potatoes, mushy peas, tartar sauce, and a wedge of lemon or splash of malt vinegar.

Smoked haddock hash with cornichon crème fraîche and salmon caviar

Serves 2 as a light lunch or 4 as a starter

Preparation time: 10 minutes

Cooking time: 25 minutes

If you cook in the same style as me, you probably verge on the overgenerous side of portion control. So more often than not you are left with plenty of leftovers. A hash is the perfect way of making sure none of that goes to waste and making leftovers go a bit further. I had a delicious hash at a small café in East London; it was a ham hock hash topped with a sunshine-orange fried egg. I've swapped ham for smoky haddock and the standard egg for some salmon caviar that pops in your mouth. But feel free to experiment with whatever is left in your refrigerator.

1 tbsp olive oil

1 onion, peeled and finely chopped

2 potatoes, scrubbed clean and cut into ⅜-in cubes

pinch of sea salt

5 oz smoked haddock, skin removed, flesh coarsely chopped

freshly ground black pepper

6 cornichons, finely chopped

3 tbsp crème fraîche

1 tsp lemon juice

¼ cup salmon caviar

2 tbsp finely chopped chives

Heat the oil in a large frying pan over medium heat. Once the oil is hot, add the onion, potatoes, and salt. Sauté, stirring every so often, for 20 minutes, or until the potatoes are tender. Add the haddock and fry for 5 minutes. Remove from the heat and season with plenty of pepper.

In the meantime, mix the cornichons with the crème fraîche and lemon juice. Divide the potato mixture between plates. Dot the cornichon–crème fraîche and 1 to 2 tbsp salmon caviar on top of the hash. Sprinkle with chives and serve.

Tip
Other smoked fish, such as mackerel, may be substituted for the smoked haddock. If using smoked salmon, omit it from the cooking process, cut it into ribbons, and use as a garnish.

Speedy one-pot noodle

Serves
1

Preparation time:
3 minutes

Inspired by the classic Pot Noodle (otherwise known as Cup Noodles), this recipe is a gourmet version of the fastest of foods. You can jazz up this simple bowl of broth and noodles with all manner of meats and vegetables, then accessorize with fresh herbs, spices, and seasonings. Here you have it: lunch in 3 minutes.

2 to 3 cubes frozen reduced ham stock (see page 248)

½ oz rice vermicelli noodles, broken up and soaked in boiling water for 1 minute, then drained

1 oz smoked tofu, sliced

3 fresh shiitake mushrooms, sliced

2 canned baby corn cobs, chopped

¾ cup boiling water

½ small red chile, seeded and sliced

1 tbsp chopped cilantro or alfalfa and radish sprouts

2 green onions, thinly sliced

pinch of togarashi* or red pepper flakes (optional)

1 lime wedge

fish sauce for serving

light soy sauce for serving

* a Japanese seasoning with chile, orange, seaweed, and sesame seeds

Place the ham stock, noodles, tofu, mushrooms, and baby corn in a serving bowl, then pour the boiling water over to cover. Mix well and add the chile, cilantro, green onions, and togarashi. Serve with a squeeze of lime, and fish sauce and soy sauce.

Variation
¾ cup hot vegetable stock

½ oz rice vermicelli noodles, broken up and soaked in boiling water for 1 minute, then drained

1 tbsp tomato purée

1 tbsp Thai green curry paste

⅓ cup broccoli florets, blanched

⅓ cup shredded roast chicken

⅓ cup shredded red cabbage

Provençal roast chicken with roasted fennel

Serves 4	Preparation time: 20 minutes	Resting time: 15 to 20 minutes	Cooking time: 1 hour 20 minutes

A Sunday roast was a ritual in my house when I was a kid. My mum would spend ages in the kitchen preparing everything and making it perfect. The roasting smells wafting from the oven always made my stomach rumble.

This particular version was inspired by a visit to Provence, where olives sneak their way into numerous dishes (tapenade, *salade niçoise, pissaladière*) and the influence of nearby North Africa has introduced preserved lemons and the sweetness of golden raisins to savory dishes. This stuffing is an amalgamation of these flavors and makes for an effortlessly succulent roast chicken.

For the seasoning

½ cup pitted green olives

5 preserved lemons, drained, halved, and seeded

2 cloves of garlic, peeled

¼ cup fresh flat-leaf parsley leaves

pinch of sea salt

freshly ground pepper

one 3-lb whole free-range chicken (see tip)

4 bulbs fennel, quartered, tough stems removed

2 onions, peeled and quartered

½ cup golden raisins

¾ cup white wine

knob of soft butter

flaky sea salt

Bean Salad (page 45)

Preheat the oven to 350°F.

To make the seasoning: In a food processor, process the olives, preserved lemons, garlic, parsley, sea salt, and a sprinkling of pepper to a paste.

With your fingers, gently loosen the skin above the breast and legs of the chicken, keeping the skin intact but creating enough space to slip the seasoning all the way under. Spread the seasoning over the chicken under the skin.

Place the fennel and onions in a large roasting pan and scatter the raisins over the top. Pour the wine into the pan. Place the chicken directly on top of the vegetables.

Rub the butter into the chicken skin and scatter some flaky salt over the top. Roast the chicken breast-side up for 1 hour 20 minutes.

Remove the pan from the oven and let the chicken rest for 10 to 15 minutes before transferring to a board to carve.

Serve the chicken with the braised fennel and onions from the pan, spooning over some of the pan juices (these are lovely and you don't want to waste them). Serve with the bean salad.

Tip

If you have a larger or smaller than 3-lb chicken, work out the cooking time for your bird based on this rule of thumb: 20 minutes per 1 lb, plus 20 minutes.

Butternut snails with baby spinach and crispy ground lamb

Serves	Preparation time:	Cooking time:
4	30 minutes	40 minutes

When I visited the Princes' Islands in Turkey, I met a lady named Buket, who runs a charming little bohemian café. Her kitchen is as tiny as the one I had in Paris, but she still manages to rustle up delicious treats for her customers. She also proves that you don't need an oven to make fantastic pastries. My version looks more like snails, and boasts a hearty filling of butternut squash.

2 tbsp olive or vegetable oil

3 onions, peeled and finely chopped

12 oz butternut squash, peeled, seeded, and cut into ½-in cubes

zest of ½ orange

¼ tsp dried thyme

pinch of ground cinnamon

sea salt and freshly ground pepper

1 handful of fresh baby spinach

1 egg

1 tbsp milk

8 large sheets filo pastry

For the crispy lamb

3 oz ground lamb

1 tbsp sumac

½ tsp red pepper flakes

1 tbsp olive or vegetable oil

For the yogurt dressing

½ cup plus 2 tbsp plain yogurt

zest and juice of ½ orange

pinch of granulated sugar

sea salt and freshly ground pepper

1 large handful of fresh baby spinach

Heat 1 tbsp of the oil in a large frying pan over high heat. Add the onions and fry for 5 minutes, then add the butternut squash, orange zest, thyme, and cinnamon. Season with salt and pepper, cover, turn the heat to low, and cook for 15 minutes, or until the squash is tender and the onions are soft. Throw in the spinach and stir; cover again and cook for 1 minute to wilt the spinach. Tip the filling onto a large plate and set it aside to cool completely.

Whisk the egg and milk together to make an egg wash. Unroll a sheet of filo pastry horizontally on your work surface, keeping the remaining sheets covered with a damp kitchen towel. Brush the filo with the egg wash, then put another sheet on top. Place one-fourth of the squash filling in a thin line horizontally, about 1½ in from the edge of the sheet, then start rolling the filo over the filling to cover. When you have a long, snakelike roll, roll it into a spiral to make a snail shape. Repeat with the rest of the filo to make four snails in total.

Heat the remaining 1 tbsp oil in a large nonstick frying pan over medium-low heat. Place the filo snails in the pan and cook for 15 minutes, flipping over after 4 to 8 minutes. The snails should be nicely crisp on both sides. Transfer to a plate and cover with aluminum foil to keep warm.

To make the crispy lamb: Mix together the lamb, sumac, and red pepper flakes. Wipe out the pan, add the oil, and place over high heat. When the oil begins to smoke, add the lamb mixture and turn the heat to medium-high. Mash the mixture with a wooden spoon to break it up and cook for 4 minutes, or until crisp.

To make the yogurt dressing: Whisk together the yogurt, orange juice, orange zest, and sugar. Season with salt and pepper.

Place a snail on a plate. Top with a small heap of baby spinach. Drizzle with the dressing and sprinkle with the crispy lamb. Serve immediately.

Tips

Wrap the snails really carefully in plastic wrap if you are making them in advance, to stop the filo from drying out.

If you can't find sumac, replace with some fresh lemon zest and a pinch of paprika.

Get ahead

You can make the snails a few hours before serving, then just reheat in the oven at 300°F for 20 minutes.

Sticky chicken with Malaysian salad

Serves	Preparation time:	Cooking time:
4	30 minutes	45 minutes

Cucumber and pineapple make a traditional Malaysian salad, or *kerabu*, although it usually includes a fiery chile. I took out the chile so that the salad's cooling properties balance the spiciness of the chicken. The last time I had the salad was at the Malaysian Hall canteen in London, where homesick Malay students go to get their fill of home-cooking, just like mum makes it. The salad was so spicy it left my mouth numb.

For the glaze

3 cloves of garlic, peeled

One 1¼-in piece ginger, peeled and coarsely chopped

⅓ cup runny honey

⅓ cup light soy sauce or tamari

1 red chile, with seeds

2 tbsp sesame oil

2 tbsp fish sauce

2 lb chicken drumsticks and thighs (4 of each)

1 tbsp sesame seeds, toasted

For the Malaysian salad

1 cucumber

½ small pineapple

1 small red onion

juice of 1 lime

sea salt

Preheat the oven to 400°F.

To make the glaze: In a food processor, blend all the ingredients together until fairly smooth.

Place the chicken pieces in a large roasting pan with the glaze, tossing them well to coat. Bake for 45 minutes, remove from the oven, and sprinkle with the toasted sesame seeds.

To make the Malaysian salad: Halve the cucumber lengthwise, then seed with a spoon and discard the seeds. Cut in half again, then slice on an angle and put in a large bowl. Peel the pineapple, cut into small cubes, and add to the bowl. Peel and thinly slice the onion. Add to the bowl, along with the lime juice.

Taste and season the salad with salt just before serving alongside the chicken.

Tips

If you want to bulk up the meal, serve with cooked basmati rice.

Season the salad with salt just before serving because if it's seasoned too far in advance, the salt will draw the moisture out of the cucumber, making the salad watery.

Get ahead

The uncooked chicken can be left in the glaze in the refrigerator for up to 2 days before baking.

Venison steak with celeriac purée, pickled blackberries, and carrot petals

Serves	Preparation time:	Cooking time:
4	20 minutes	30 minutes

I have spent a great deal of time in Sweden over the last few years and developed an affinity for the flavors of the land. Sweden's long, cold winters have had a considerable impact on the national cuisine, bringing an abundance of root vegetables and game meat into the diet and also influencing culinary techniques, such as pickling and smoking, which help preserve food throughout the year.

For the pickled blackberries and carrots

3 tbsp apple cider vinegar

½ cup granulated sugar

½ cup plus 2 tbsp water

1 tbsp sea salt

5 juniper berries, lightly crushed

10 peppercorns

1⅔ cups blackberries

2 small carrots

For the celeriac purée

1 celeriac, peeled

3 or 4 parsnips

2 tbsp vegetable oil

6 to 10 tbsp milk

2 knobs of soft butter

pinch of freshly ground nutmeg

½ tsp white pepper

sea salt

1 tbsp oil

1 lb 2 oz venison fillet steaks (1¼ in thick)

sea salt and freshly ground black pepper

1 handful of mixed fresh herbs, such as flat-leaf parsley, chives, or dill, chopped

To make the pickled blackberries and carrots: In a medium saucepan over medium-high heat, stir together the vinegar, sugar, water, salt, juniper berries, and peppercorns and slowly bring to a boil. Once the sugar and salt have dissolved, 1 to 2 minutes, remove from the heat and let cool for 5 minutes. Add the blackberries and set aside. Peel the carrots and use a mandoline to make wafer-thin horizontal petals, or cut the carrots in half vertically and shave off petals with a peeler. Place the carrots in a small bowl, add 2 tbsp of the pickling liquid, and toss. Set aside.

To make the celeriac purée: Cut the celeriac and parsnips into ½-in cubes. Throw them into a medium saucepan with the oil, stir, and place over medium heat. Cover tightly and cook for 15 to 20 minutes, or until tender, stirring regularly. Transfer to a food processor and blend with the milk, starting with 6 tbsp and adding 2 tbsp at a time, then the butter. Add the nutmeg and white pepper and mix well. Season with salt.

Preheat the oven to 300°F. Put a large ovenproof frying pan over medium-high heat.

Rub the oil all over the steaks and season them with salt and pepper. Place the steaks in the hot pan and cook for 1½ to 2 minutes on each side, or until they have a lovely dark crust.

Transfer the pan to the oven for 5 minutes for medium doneness. Place your serving plates in the oven at the same time to warm.

Take the steaks out of the oven. Cover with aluminum foil and set aside to rest for 5 minutes, then transfer to a cutting board and cut into thin slices.

Put a generous dollop of purée on each plate, followed by several slices of venison and a little of the meat juices. Finish by spooning the pickled blackberries and carrots on top and around the plate. Garnish with the herbs before serving.

Tips

Take the steaks out of the refrigerator at least 30 minutes before cooking them.

Cooking the celeriac with no water and only a little oil allows it to cook in its own juices. (There's no water to dilute the taste.) Pass the purée through a sieve or ricer for an extra-smooth texture.

Get ahead

The pickled blackberries will keep in an air-tight container or jar in the refrigerator for up to 2 weeks.

Shepherdless pie

Serves
4 to 6

Preparation time:
30 minutes

Cooking time:
40 minutes

Shepherd's pie is one of my favorite British dishes, and I often made it in my days au pair-ing for a French family in Paris. I've adapted it by using Puy lentils, from the Auvergne region in France; they keep their shape and have a great bite, making them a perfect substitute for ground meat.

Making shepherd's pie can be a bit time-consuming if you have to make mashed potatoes (although it's a great way to use leftovers). So I've simplified it by using a creamy polenta topping that is crisped up in the oven—meaning less time in the kitchen and more time to put your feet up (or get all those other tasks done).

For the filling

1 cup dried Puy or beluga lentils

2 Lapsang souchong tea bags

4½ cups cold water

1 tbsp canola or olive oil

1 onion, peeled and finely chopped

1 carrot, peeled and diced

10 cherry tomatoes, finely chopped

1 tbsp sweet smoked paprika

8 mushrooms, coarsely chopped

2 tbsp tomato purée

2 tsp Marmite or yeast extract

sea salt and freshly ground pepper

For the creamy polenta topping

3¾ cups vegetable stock

1 tbsp fresh thyme leaves

1 tbsp finely chopped fresh parsley

1½ cups instant polenta

1 tbsp canola or olive oil

To make the filling: Place the lentils and tea bags in a medium saucepan. Cover with the cold water and bring to a boil, then lower the heat and simmer for 20 to 25 minutes or until the lentils are al dente. Drain the lentils, saving ¾ cup of the cooking liquid, and discard the tea bags.

Preheat the broiler.

Put the oil into a large frying pan and add the onion, carrot, tomatoes, and paprika. Fry gently for 10 minutes, or until the onion is translucent. Add the mushrooms and cook for 5 minutes more, stirring frequently.

Add the cooked lentils and the reserved cooking liquid, the tomato purée, and Marmite. Stir until the tomato purée and Marmite have dissolved, then cook for 2 minutes. Taste and season with salt and pepper. Remove from the heat and cover while making the polenta.

To make the creamy polenta topping: Put the stock and herbs in a large saucepan and bring to a boil. Add the polenta in a slow stream, stirring continuously for a couple of minutes until the mixture thickens and bubbles. Stir in the oil and remove from the heat. Taste for seasoning.

Pour the lentil filling into a baking dish and spread the hot polenta over the top. Use a fork to make lines in the top; this helps to make it crispier. Place under the broiler for 3 to 5 minutes, or until the top crisps up. Serve immediately.

Tip

Stir the polenta continuously with a wooden spoon or large balloon whisk to prevent lumps from forming. If it is thickening too quickly, remove from the heat and beat vigorously.

Cauliflower cheese burgers

Serves
6

Preparation time:
20 minutes

Cooking time:
25 minutes

The burger craze doesn't seem to have left a stone unturned. New York, London, Paris, Stockholm—every city I visit has any number of burger bars touting gourmet beef patties in soft brioche buns. Don't get me wrong, I love a burger! But after seeing all that meat I find myself craving something a little lighter and fresher tasting. Wrap your hand round this cauliflower cheese burger, take a big bite and let some of the juice dribble down your hand . . . just like the real deal!

For the caramelized onion chutney

¼ cup butter

4 red onions, peeled and thinly sliced

pinch of sea salt

½ cup plus 2 tbsp red wine vinegar

2 tbsp raisins, finely chopped

2 tbsp light brown sugar

1 very small head cauliflower, trimmed and separated into florets

1¼ cups drained canned navy beans

¾ cup fresh bread crumbs

5 oz mature Cheddar cheese

2 tbsp chopped fresh flat-leaf parsley

sprinkling of grated nutmeg

zest of 1 unwaxed lemon

1 tbsp chopped toasted hazelnuts

sea salt and freshly ground pepper

1 egg white

2 tbsp vegetable or olive oil

1 head oak leaf or other leaf lettuce

1 tomato, sliced

To make the caramelized onion chutney: Melt the butter in a frying pan over low heat, then add the onions and salt. Sauté for about 20 minutes, or until sticky and soft. Add the vinegar, raisins, and brown sugar, and cook for another 5 minutes, or until glossy and reduced. Taste and adjust the seasoning, if needed. Set aside.

Steam the cauliflower florets for 7 to 8 minutes, or until tender. Remove from the heat, drain, and leave in the colander to cool.

When the cauliflower is cool, put the navy beans in a food processor and pulse, then add the cauliflower and pulse lightly. You don't want to overwork or the mixture will get sloppy. Transfer to a bowl and add 1 tbsp of the bread crumbs. Grate a little more than half of the Cheddar and add it to the bowl, along with the parsley, nutmeg, lemon zest, and hazelnuts. Season with salt and pepper. Using the palms of your hands, form the mix into six 2½-in round patties.

Lightly whisk the egg white in a bowl, and put the rest of the bread crumbs on a plate. Brush each patty all over with egg white and press into the crumbs, making sure each patty is well covered.

Heat the oil into a large frying pan over medium-high heat. Cook the patties in batches for 3 to 4 minutes on each side, until crisp and golden. Slice the remaining Cheddar and put a slice on top of each patty while in the pan to melt. Place each patty in a lettuce leaf, add a slice of tomato, and serve with a generous spoonful of chutney.

Tip

Serve with toasted pita bread or on a brioche bun if you want a more classic burger.

Get ahead

Once formed, you can freeze the patties on a tray until firm, then transfer to a resealable bag and store in the freezer. Then defrost, coat in egg white and bread crumbs, and fry as directed.

Duck ragù with crisp porridge wedges

Serves	Preparation time:	Cooking time:	Chilling time:
4	30 minutes	2 hours	30 minutes

I have an enduring love of porridge and it doesn't stop at breakfast. I grew up with savory porridge for dinner. My mum, an ever-so-thrifty cook, made an Asian-style porridge using leftover rice and roast chicken, spiked with chile, ginger, and green onions. Serving porridge for dinner might not be the most obvious choice, but panfry it to crisp and golden perfection and you'll end up with the most amazing accompaniment to a rich ragù.

For the orange-duck ragù

3 duck legs

sea salt and freshly ground pepper

1 tbsp sunflower oil

4 cloves of garlic, peeled and finely minced

2 anchovy fillets, drained and chopped

1 onion, peeled and finely chopped

2 carrots, peeled and roughly chopped

1 stalk celery, coarsely chopped

½ cup plus 2 tbsp red wine

one 15-oz can cherry tomatoes

1 large sprig of rosemary

zest of 1 orange, removed in strips using a vegetable peeler

For the crisp porridge wedges

1½ cups rolled oats

1 cup milk

1½ cups hot chicken stock

3 tbsp finely chopped chives

¾ cup finely grated Parmesan cheese

1 tbsp butter

To make the ragù: Season the duck legs with plenty of salt and pepper. Heat the oil in a large lidded saucepan over medium heat. Place the duck legs in the pan, skin-side down, and fry for 3 minutes, or until the skin begins to turn golden and crisp. Flip and cook for 2 minutes more. Remove from the pan and place on a plate.

Lower the heat and add the garlic, anchovies, onion, carrots, and celery. Fry for about 5 minutes, or until the anchovies have disintegrated, then add the wine. Simmer for 2 minutes, then add the tomatoes, rosemary, and orange zest. Return to a simmer, add the browned duck legs, cover, and cook for about 1½ hours, or until the meat is tender and falling off the bone. Discard the orange zest and rosemary. Transfer the duck legs to a cutting board and, using two forks, shred the meat, discarding the skin and bones. Stir the duck meat back into the tomato sauce, taste, and adjust the seasonings if necessary.

To make the crisp porridge wedges: Line an 8-in-square pan with plastic wrap. Place the oats in a medium saucepan with the milk and stock. Let soak for 10 minutes, then bring to a simmer over medium-low heat, stirring continously with a wooden spoon or spatula. When the porridge is thick, remove it from the heat. Stir in most of the chives (saving some for garnish), the Parmesan, and some salt and pepper and stir well to combine. Pour the porridge into the prepared pan and spread evenly. Refrigerate for at least 30 minutes. Invert the pan onto a cutting board, peel away the plastic wrap, and cut the porridge into quarters.

Melt 1 tbsp of the butter in a large frying pan over high heat. Fry the porridge squares until golden on both sides, 6 to 7 minutes.

Place a porridge square on each serving plate and top with the ragù and a sprinkle of the remaining chives. Serve immediately.

Stir-fried cauliflower rice

Serves 4

Preparation time: 20 minutes

Cooking time: 10 minutes

I'm a firm believer in the mantra "butter makes everything better," but there are some days when I fancy something a touch lighter. True to my Asian roots, I regularly rustle up a stir-fry from a fridge raid of leftovers when I want a quick bite; using cauliflower as a rice substitute makes the dish even healthier.

I small head cauliflower, trimmed and separated into florets

4 green onions, white and green parts separated and finely chopped

10 baby corn, cut into rounds

I red bell pepper, seeded and cut into thin strips

2 tbsp sunflower oil

4 eggs

pinch of white pepper

pinch of sea salt

I red chile, seeded and finely chopped

4 cloves of garlic, peeled and finely minced

I thumb-size piece fresh ginger, peeled and grated

¼ cup cashew nuts, coarsely chopped

¼ cup light soy sauce or tamari

I lime, quartered

Place the cauliflower in a blender or food processor and pulse until it's the consistency of bread crumbs. Transfer to a bowl; add the white parts of the green onions, the baby corn, and bell pepper; and mix.

Place a large nonstick frying pan over medium heat and add I tbsp of the oil. Crack the eggs into a bowl and beat with the white pepper and salt. Pour the eggs into the pan and swirl the pan around, so the mixture covers the whole base. Cook for a couple of minutes, or until the eggs are set, then flip the eggs and cook for 1 to 2 minutes, or until just set. Slide the eggs onto a cutting board and let cool slightly. When cool enough to handle, roll up and cut into ½-in-wide strips. Set aside until needed.

Heat the remaining I tbsp oil in a wok or large frying pan over medium heat. Add the chile, garlic, ginger, and cashews. Cook for 30 seconds while continuously tossing in the hot oil. Add the cauliflower, corn, and bell pepper. Continue tossing for 3 to 4 minutes, until it's nicely golden. Add the sliced egg and stir to heat through, then pour the soy sauce into the pan and toss well before dividing between bowls. Serve each with a wedge of lime and sprinkling of the green onion tops.

Tips

Use a teaspoon to scrape the skin off the ginger.

Use tamari instead of regular soy sauce to make this gluten-free.

Stir-frying is an excellent way to use up anything left over in the refrigerator, from roast meat to vegetables.

Mushroom stroganoff with spinach and wild rice

Preparation time:
15 minutes

Cooking time:
30 minutes

I have a fond memory of stroganoff, since it was often served for dinner at home when I was a kid. My mum has always been a classic cook, so we had beef stroganoff rather than my vegetarian version. Portobello mushrooms are a popular meat substitute in vegetarian cooking; they are dense and chewy and have a deep, intense flavor. I think they can match beef or chicken any day, and for a fraction of the price.

1 cup wild red rice (I like Camargue)

1 handful of baby spinach

1 tbsp butter

4 extra-large portobello mushrooms, stemmed

3 cloves of garlic, peeled and minced

1⅔ cups vegetable stock

2 tsp cornstarch

2 tbsp whole milk, plus ½ cup

2 tbsp Dijon mustard

freshly ground pepper

juice and zest of ½ unwaxed lemon

heaping 2 tbsp cornichons, finely chopped

2 sprigs of dill, finely chopped

Cook the wild rice in salted boiling water in a medium saucepan according to the package instructions. Drain and return to the pan with the baby spinach. Stir so the spinach wilts, then cover and set aside until needed.

Put the butter in a large frying pan over medium heat. Add the mushrooms with the flat caps facing down and sauté until soft and beginning to brown. Flip them over and cook for several minutes, then add the garlic. Place the stock in a medium saucepan over medium heat and bring to a simmer.

In a separate bowl, mix the cornstarch with the 2 tbsp milk to make a smooth paste. Whisk it into the hot stock, along with the Dijon mustard and remaining ½ cup milk. Season with pepper. Add it to the mushrooms (beware, as it may sputter). Simmer for 2 minutes, then remove the mushrooms from the pan and set aside, covering them with aluminum foil to keep warm. Turn the heat to medium-high and whisk the sauce as it cooks for about 15 minutes, or until it has the consistency of heavy cream. Remove from the heat, squeeze in the lemon juice, and taste and adjust for seasoning, if necessary.

Serve each mushroom on a bed of spinach wild rice. Spoon the sauce over the top and garnish with the cornichons, lemon zest, and dill.

Tip
The mushrooms can be replaced with 1½ lb of beef or chicken. Cut into thin strips or bite-size pieces and sauté for about 10 minutes, stirring regularly. Proceed as directed.

Get ahead
You can make the sauce and sauté the mushrooms in advance, then reheat over low heat.

Chicken salad with buttermilk dressing and chicken skin croutons

Serves	Preparation time:	Cooking time:
4	15 minutes	35 minutes

Iceberg lettuce went out of fashion some time ago, losing to a bag of prewashed mixed leaves. But it's definitely making a comeback. Wedges of iceberg are now popping up on restaurant menus, reminding us that there's something ever so refreshing about the crunchy fresh lettuce that no spindly arugula leaf, radicchio, or baby red chard can fulfill. This is my salad of choice on a hot day.

6 tbsp water

½ cup granulated sugar

1 lemon, thinly sliced and seeded

2 large skin-on chicken breasts

sea salt

4 tsp Dijon mustard

2 tsp canola oil

6 tbsp buttermilk

1 small clove of garlic, peeled

4 anchovy fillets, drained

2 stalks celery, trimmed

1 head iceberg lettuce, quartered and washed

½ cucumber, thinly sliced into rounds

2 tbsp finely chopped chives

2 tbsp capers, drained (rinsed if salted)

Preheat the oven to 400°F. Line a baking sheet with parchment paper. Place the water and sugar in a medium saucepan over high heat and bring to a boil. Place the lemon slices in a heatproof bowl. Once the sugar has dissolved and the syrup has boiled for 1 minute, pour it over the lemon. Set aside to cool until needed.

Remove the skin from the chicken breasts. Place the skin on the prepared baking sheet, sprinkle with salt, and bake for 30 minutes, or until golden and crisp. Remove from the sheet and place on a cutting board. Cut into small pieces.

Meanwhile, heat a griddle pan until very hot. Butterfly the chicken breasts by placing on a cutting board, then using a sharp knife to slice each one horizontally, starting from the straighter side. Don't cut all the way through; leave one side intact, so you can open up each breast like a book. Set aside on a plate, then take two pieces of plastic wrap that are three times larger than an open fillet. Lay one piece of plastic wrap on the board, place an open fillet on top, and cover with the second piece of plastic wrap. Use a rolling pin to pound the chicken to about ¼ in thick. Repeat with the other fillet.

Remove the chicken from the plastic wrap. Spread the Dijon mustard on both sides, drizzle with the oil, and sprinkle with salt. Place one fillet on the griddle pan once it's smoking hot and sear for 2 minutes on each side. Transfer the chicken to a clean cutting board. Repeat with the other fillet. Let the chicken rest for 5 minutes, and then slice into thin strips.

Blend the buttermilk, garlic, and anchovies using an immersion blender or a food processor. Using a peeler, make ribbons from the celery stalks. Divide the iceberg lettuce among shallow bowls. Add the strips of chicken, cucumber, and celery, then drizzle with the buttermilk dressing. Sprinkle with the crispy chicken skin, chives, capers, and some of the drained candied lemon slices.

Tip

This dish also makes a great side salad if you leave the chicken out and slice the iceberg lettuce into strips.

Get ahead

The candied lemon slices can be made up to 1 week in advance and stored in an airtight container in the refrigerator. You can substitute them, finely sliced, for preserved lemons in other recipes.

Onion petal spätzle

Preparation time:
15 minutes

Cooking time:
60 minutes

Spätzle—little button dumplings—are something I grew up with, having an Austrian mum. They're usually tossed in butter and served with grated cheese, but I serve them with dry-roasted onions, which gives the dish a lovely sweetness. This technique is inspired by our Nordic gastro-trendsetters, who know a thing or two about alliums.

6 yellow onions, unpeeled and quartered

8 garlic cloves, unpeeled

3 tbsp soft butter, plus a knob for frying

2 shallots, quartered

2 eggs

1 cup fresh parsley leaves

sea salt and freshly ground pepper

1 cup plus 2 tbsp all-purpose flour

1 handful of chopped mixed fresh herbs such as parsley, thyme, oregano, and basil

½ cup grated Parmesan or other mature hard cheese

Preheat the oven to 350°F.

Place the onions and 6 cloves of the garlic skin-side down in a roasting pan. Roast for 30 minutes, or until soft and golden.

Peel the remaining 2 garlic cloves and put them in a food processor, along with the butter, shallots, eggs, parsley, ½ tsp salt, and ½ tsp pepper. Blend to a smooth paste, remove from the blender, and beat in the flour.

Place a colander on top of a saucepan of simmering salted water (don't let the colander touch the water). Pour in the batter and use a spatula to push it through the holes, making *spätzle*. Cook for 2 minutes, then drain.

Peel the roasted onions and cut off the root ends, then pull the onion layers apart, into petals. Put the knob of butter into a large frying pan over medium heat. When the butter has melted, turn the heat to low and add the herbs and onion petals. Squeeze the roasted garlic into the pan, discarding the skins. When the butter begins to brown, remove from the heat and add the *spätzle*, tossing to coat. Season, then scatter the cheese on top and serve immediately.

Tips

If you don't have any fresh herbs, you can use 1 tbsp dried herbs instead.

If you have some white wine left over (roughly 6 tbsp), add it to the pan before adding the spätzle. Turn up the heat and reduce by half, then add the spätzle.

Get ahead

The onions and garlic can be roasted in advance and heated in the pan with the butter.

Pickled pear, lentil, and gorgonzola salad

Serves	Preparation time:	Resting time:	Cooking time:
4	15 minutes	overnight	1 hour

The wholesome image that lentils conjure up always leaves me with a smug glow in the aftermath of eating—quite unlike pasta or rice, which can leave you feeling bloated. After living in France, there's only one kind of lentil I like to eat (call me a lentil snob if you like), and that's the Puy. It keeps its shape and doesn't end up mushy. Puy lentils are easy to top with an endless combination of ingredients or can be thrown into a salad to give it some bite. Don't let your lentils get pushed to the back of the cupboard!

I cup water

I cup red wine vinegar

¾ cup granulated sugar

4 firm pears, peeled but with the stems on

4 small beets, peeled and cut into ¾-in cubes

I cup Puy lentils

3½ oz Gorgonzola or other blue cheese

I handful of watercress

2 tbsp extra-virgin olive oil

pinch of sea salt

pinch of freshly ground pepper

Put the water, vinegar, and sugar in a medium saucepan (just big enough for the pears to nest in snugly) and bring to a gentle simmer over low heat. Stir to dissolve the sugar, then add the pears and beets. Cut a piece of parchment paper larger than the diameter of the pan, crumple it up, and cut a hole or slit in the center. Place in contact with the liquid and let some seep through to keep the paper in place. Cover and simmer gently over low heat for I hour.

Remove from the heat and transfer the pears, beets, and all the liquid to a lidded container. Set aside to cool to room temperature, then put in the refrigerator to pickle overnight.

When ready to serve, cook the lentils following the package instructions, then drain. Transfer the pears to a cutting board and the beets to a bowl (discard the liquid or save it for up to I week for pickling something else). Toss the lentils with the beets, then crumble the blue cheese into small chunks and add to the bowl.

Divide the mixture among four salad plates. Cut each pear in half and place two halves on each plate, with a little watercress on top. Drizzle with the oil and sprinkle with the salt and pepper.

Tips

It's important that the pears are large, firm, and not overripe; otherwise, they will become mushy and disintegrate when cooked.

You can use any other soft cheese, such as goat's cheese or feta, to replace the blue cheese.

Get ahead

The longer the pears and beets sit in the pickling juices, the darker the color and the stronger the flavor.

Chicory, blood orange, and scallop salad

Serves
2 as a light lunch
or 4 as a starter

Preparation time:
10 minutes

Cooking time:
under 5 minutes

I love a colorful plate of food, especially on a dreary winter's day. Luckily, even in the winter months you can add some color to your plate with red chicory and blood oranges. They just happen to be in season at the same time, and there couldn't be a better match. Bitter chicory and sweet-and-sour blood oranges are not just the ultimate color combo but a perfect palate pairing too.

4 blood oranges

2 tbsp extra-virgin olive oil

2 heads red chicory, ends trimmed and leaves separated

sea salt and freshly ground pepper

8 scallops with roe, at room temperature for 15 minutes before cooking

1 tbsp olive oil

1 tbsp butter

20 green olives, pitted and finely chopped

2 tbsp finely chopped chives

Using a paring knife, cut the tops and bottoms off the oranges. Set upright on the cutting board and slice away the skin and pith, working around the oranges. Cut between the membranes to remove the individual segments of orange, then place in a bowl. Squeeze the juice from the remaining membranes into a salad bowl.

Add the extra-virgin olive oil to the orange juice in the salad bowl and whisk. Add the chicory leaves, toss to dress, and season with salt and pepper.

Peel away the tough crescent-shaped tendon from the outside of the scallops. Dab the scallops with a paper towel to remove any moisture and season well with salt and pepper on both sides.

Put a large nonstick frying pan over medium heat and pour in the olive oil. When the pan is hot, add the scallops. Sear on the first side for 1 to 2 minutes (depending on their size) without disturbing them, so that they get a nice crust. Then add the butter to the pan, flip the scallops over, and cook for 1 minute more, tilting the pan and spooning the butter over the scallops.

Scatter the chicory leaves on a serving platter or individual plates, followed by the orange segments and the olives. Place the scallops on top and sprinkle with the chives before serving.

Tip
The scallops can be replaced with 3½ oz of salty, creamy goat's cheese.

Get ahead
You can segment the oranges and make the dressing a few hours in advance.

Summer spaghetti bolognese

Serves	Preparation time:	Cooking time:
4	15 minutes	15 minutes

There are a few things I try to grow in my window boxes, and herbs, radishes, and lettuce are a must. One year I grew cherry tomatoes, which proved such a success that I couldn't pick them quickly enough. My neighbors complained that tomatoes would fall on their heads when they walked into the main entrance below. I didn't intend to bomb my neighbors with tomatoes, so now I keep my urban gardening to herbs and leafy greens, which are easy to maintain. This recipe really relies on a bounty of summer tomatoes to bring it alive. Unlike the classic spaghetti Bolognese, which benefits from a slow, gentle simmer, this is a quick, fresh alternative.

I lb mixed tomatoes (different colors and sizes)

I small red onion, peeled and thinly sliced

I tbsp extra-virgin olive oil

2 tbsp canola oil

I yellow onion, peeled and finely chopped

4 cloves of garlic, peeled and crushed

7 oz lamb's liver, finely chopped

8 slices bacon, finely chopped

I tbsp chopped fresh thyme leaves, plus more for garnish

I tbsp chopped fresh oregano leaves, plus more for garnish

I lb spaghetti

I tbsp tomato paste

3 tbsp red wine vinegar

sea salt and freshly ground pepper

Quarter or halve the tomatoes, depending on their size. Toss with the red onion and extra-virgin olive oil and set aside.

Put the canola oil, yellow onion, garlic, liver, and bacon in a large frying pan over medium heat. Add the herbs and sauté, stirring continuously, for 10 minutes, or until the onion and meat begin to brown nicely.

Bring a large pot of salted water to a boil. Add the spaghetti and cook according to the package instructions. When cooked, drain in a colander, reserving about ¼ cup of the pasta water. Return the pasta to the pot and stir in the tomato paste and red wine vinegar. Taste and season with salt and pepper.

Toss the liver and bacon with the tomatoes and pasta and loosen with 1 to 2 tbsp of the pasta water. Pour into a large serving dish, sprinkle the additional herbs on top, and serve immediately.

Tip
The liver and bacon can be replaced with ground beef, lamb, or pork.

Get ahead
The liver and onion mixture can be made a day ahead. Simply reheat in a pan with 1 tbsp oil.

Zucchini linguine with three different sauces

Serves	Preparation time:	Cooking time:
4	10 minutes	15 minutes

I'm one to break the rules, and when it comes to pasta I say no to flour and yes to vegetables. Homemade pasta doesn't have to contain flour or be tricky to make, and zucchini linguine is perfect for your gluten-intolerant friends. All you need is some zucchini and a julienne peeler, spiralizer, or mandoline.

I returned from my travels craving vegetables and something a little lighter. I can be pretty lazy when it comes to cooking for myself, and these pasta dishes can all be rustled up in minutes.

Tip
Zucchini linguine is best eaten immediately, as it gets soggy if you reheat it.

Get ahead
The three sauces can all be made up to 2 days in advance.

with frozen pea and dill pesto

5 oz frozen petit pois or garden peas

4 sprigs fresh dill

pinch of sugar

pinch of sea salt

2 tbsp water

¼ cup finely grated Parmesan cheese or other mature hard cheese, plus more for serving

2 tbsp lemon juice

freshly ground pepper

4 zucchini

1 tbsp butter

Place the peas in a small lidded saucepan. Strip the dill leaves from the stems and add the stems to the pan with the sugar and salt. Add the water, place the lid on the pan, bring to a boil, and cook for 2 minutes. Remove the lid and check the peas to be sure they are tender. If they are not, cook for 1 to 2 minutes more and then retest. Transfer to a food processor. Add the dill leaves, Parmesan, and lemon juice. Season with pepper and blend the pesto—I like to keep it a bit textured. Check the seasoning.

Using a julienne peeler, spiralizer, or a mandoline with a julienne blade, make long ribbons down the length of the zucchini, discarding the seedy center. Melt the butter in a large lidded pan over medium heat and add the zucchini. Place the lid on the pan and sweat the zucchini for 1 to 2 minutes, until softened. Drain off any excess liquid, return to the pan, and toss with the pesto. Serve with an extra grating of Parmesan.

with walnut and sage sauce

¾ cup walnuts

¼ cup salted butter, plus 1 tbsp

2 tbsp sage leaves

3 to 4 tbsp water

1 tbsp lemon juice

sea salt and freshly ground pepper

4 zucchini

Place a nonstick frying pan over a medium-high heat. When hot, put the walnuts into the pan and toast for 5 minutes, or until they smell toasted, then remove and set aside. Melt the ¼ cup butter in the pan over medium heat and add the sage leaves. Cook for about 3 minutes, or until the butter starts to brown and the leaves begin to crisp up. Transfer to a food processor. Add the toasted walnuts, water, and lemon juice. Season with salt and pepper and blend to a purée.

Using a julienne peeler, spiralizer, or a mandoline with a julienne blade, make long ribbons down the length of the zucchini, discarding the seedy center. Melt the remaining 1 tbsp butter in a large lidded pan over medium heat and add the zucchini. Place the lid on the pan and sweat the zucchini for 1 to 2 minutes, or until softened. Drain off any excess liquid, return to the pan, and toss with the walnut sauce before serving.

with tomato, olive, and caper sauce

1 tbsp olive oil

3 cloves garlic, peeled and finely minced

one 15-oz can cherry tomatoes

4 zucchini

10 black olives, pitted and chopped

2 tbsp capers, drained (rinsed if salted)

pinch of sea salt

2½ oz Parmesan cheese or other mature hard cheese

Mini Focaccia Buns (page 231)

Heat the oil in a large frying pan over a low heat. Add the garlic and sauté gently for 1 minute, then add the tomatoes with their juice and simmer for 10 minutes.

Using a julienne peeler, spiralizer, or a mandoline with a julienne blade, make long ribbons down the length of the zucchini, discarding the seedy center.

Crush the tomato sauce with a fork and stir in the olives and capers. Season with the salt, then remove from the heat and toss the zucchini in the sauce for about 1 minute, or until thoroughly coated and warmed through.

Plate the zucchini, then grate the Parmesan over the top. Serve with the mini buns to mop up the sauce.

Puff pastry pies

Makes	Preparation time:	Cooking time:
6 pie shells	15 minutes	25 to 30 minutes

If there's one thing I keep in my freezer, it's not a tub of ice cream, it's a roll of all-butter puff pastry. It's great to have as a backup for all sorts of things, from little aperitif snacks in the form of twisted cheese straws to these immensely versatile puff pastry pies.

Tip
These puff pastry pies can be filled with anything you fancy, as long as the filling isn't too wet.

two packages of ready-rolled all-butter puff pastry, at room temperature 15 minutes before using

1 egg, beaten

Preheat the oven to 350°F. Line a baking sheet with parchment paper. Unroll the pastry carefully. Cut six 4-in squares with a long knife or pizza cutter. Cut the remaining pastry into 48 strips ¾ in wide and 4 in long (you may need to reroll the last pieces for the final strips). Brush the squares with the egg, then stick a pastry strip on each edge of the squares to make a border. Top each of the borders with another layer of pastry strips, then brush again with egg and place the squares on the prepared baking sheet. Bake for 25 to 30 minutes, or until golden, crisp, and puffy.

You can make the pie shells at the same time as the fillings, or store them in an airtight container at room temperature for up to 3 days. Reheat for 15 minutes at 300°F.

Roasted baby vegetable pie filling

For 6 pies	Preparation time: 5 minutes	Cooking time: 30 minutes

12 baby zucchini

12 baby carrots

12 baby parsnips

1 tbsp olive oil

6 tsp sun-dried tomato paste

6 puff pastry pie shells (see facing page)

2 tbsp extra-virgin olive oil

sea salt

Preheat the oven to 350°F. Halve the vegetables horizontally. Put them in a small baking dish and toss with the olive oil, then roast for about 30 minutes, or until tender.

Smear the sun-dried tomato paste on the base of each pie shell. Arrange the vegetables upright in the pie shell, then drizzle with the extra-virgin olive oil and sprinkle with a little salt before serving.

Tuna, sweet corn, and caper pie filling

For 6 pies	Preparation time: 5 minutes

2 cans good-quality tuna, drained, or 5 oz smoked trout, flaked

one 8.75-oz can corn, drained

1 tbsp capers, coarsely chopped

4 cornichons, coarsely chopped

6 puff pastry pie shells (see facing page)

6 tbsp Mayonnaise (page 249)

In a small bowl, mix together the tuna, corn, capers, and cornichons. Divide among the pie shells and dot the mayonnaise on the top before serving.

continued

Roasted sausage, apple and onion pie filling

For 6 pies	Preparation time: 5 minutes	Cooking time: 30 to 40 minutes

3 small onions, peeled and quartered

6 free-range pork sausages

1 tbsp olive oil

6 apples

6 tsp English mustard

6 puff pastry pie shells (see page 140)

Preheat the oven to 350°F. Place the onions and sausages in a large roasting pan and drizzle with the oil, tossing to coat. Wrap each of the apples in a piece of aluminum foil and place in the pan. Roast for 30 to 40 minutes, or until the sausages are golden and cooked through and the onions are soft.

Remove the pan from the oven. Wearing a clean pair of rubber gloves, carefully remove the apples from the foil and mash the flesh with a fork, discarding the skin and core. Spread 1 tsp mustard in the base of each pie shell and divide the mashed apple among the shells. Cut each sausage in half and arrange in the shells, along with two onion quarters per pie. Serve immediately.

Caramelized plum filling

For 6 pies	Preparation time: 5 minutes	Cooking time: 20 minutes

knob of butter

1 tbsp light brown sugar

9 smallish plums

2 tbsp lemon juice

6 puff pastry pie shells (see page 140)

6 tbsp crème fraîche, whipped cream, or ice cream

Put a medium lidded nonstick frying pan over medium-low heat. Put the butter and sugar in the pan and let them melt for 2 minutes. Cut the plums in half, remove the pits if you can (if you can't, you can do this more easily once they are cooked), and place flesh-side down in the pan. Cook for 5 minutes, then add the lemon juice and spoon the sauce over the plums. Place a lid on the pan and cook for 10 minutes more, or until the plums are tender but still holding their shape. Place three halves in each of the pie shells and spoon over the pan juices. Serve with a dollop of crème fraîche.

Roasted baby vegetable pie filling ———

Caramelized plum filling

Tuna, sweet corn, and caper pie filling

Roasted sausage, apple, and onion pie filling

Eggplant and halloumi schnitzel
stewed tomatoes

Serves	Preparation time:	Salting time:	Cooking time:
4	10 minutes	15 minutes minimum	1 hour

Schnitzel was always a special treat at home when I was a kid. Golden crisp crumbs encasing a juicy veal escalope, with a dollop of ketchup on the side—just thinking of it makes me salivate a little. I'm not someone who believes a dinner plate is incomplete without a carnivorous centerpiece, however. The meaty texture of eggplant lends itself very well to being coated in bread crumbs and halloumi, while the stewed tomatoes are a sophisticated, grown-up homage to my childhood love of ketchup.

12 oz cherry tomatoes

2 small red onions, peeled and finely sliced

5 sprigs of fresh thyme, plus a few extra leaves for serving

2 tbsp red wine vinegar

2 tbsp extra-virgin olive oil

sea salt and freshly ground pepper

1 large globe eggplant

1 tbsp vegetable oil

1 egg

1½ cups fresh white bread crumbs

2½ oz halloumi cheese, finely grated

½ tsp dried mint

Preheat the oven to 400°F.

Place the tomatoes in a baking dish with the onions, thyme, vinegar, olive oil, and some salt and pepper. Stir well and bake for 40 minutes, giving everything another stir 20 minutes into the cooking time.

In the meantime, remove and discard the stalk from the eggplant. Slice the eggplant lengthwise into ½-in-thick slices, and slice the skin off the small end lengths (this will help the crumbs stick). Sprinkle with salt on both sides and place in a colander to drain for 15 minutes. Rinse well, then dab off the excess moisture with a paper towel.

Pour the vegetable oil into a large baking dish and place in the oven to heat. Whisk the egg and place in a shallow bowl. Mix the bread crumbs, halloumi, and dried mint together on a large plate. Set a clean plate on one side. Dip each eggplant slice into the egg, then press into the bread crumbs on both sides and place on the clean plate.

Remove the baking dish from the oven and place the eggplant slices side by side in the oil. Press any leftover crumbs onto the top of the slices. Bake for 20 to 25 minutes, or until both sides are golden and crispy.

Serve the eggplant with a dollop of the stewed tomatoes on the side and garnish with a few thyme leaves.

Tip

I like the chewy saltiness of halloumi, but you could use Parmesan or another hard cheese instead.

Teriyaki salmon steamed buns

Serves
4

Preparation time:
20 minutes

Resting time:
1 hour 15 minutes

Cooking time:
20 minutes

As a kid, getting ahold of a savory Asian bun in the suburbs of London or the Bavarian countryside was like trying to find Wi-Fi in the Sahara, so my brother and mum resorted to some DIY. Unfortunately, the result wasn't a great success and the recipe wasn't repeated. Buns were saved for when we went to Chinatown as a special treat and could chow down on a basketful. It was only years later, when I came back to London and discovered a plethora of food trucks, bun-only restaurants, and even buns on gastropub menus, that I decided it was time to have another bash at making some at home. I can assure you that you won't be needing a trip into the city after you've made these.

2 tbsp light soy sauce or tamari

2 tbsp mirin

2 tbsp runny honey

1 red chile, cut into rounds

10½ oz salmon fillets

For the bun dough

1⅓ cup all-purpose flour

1 tbsp dried nonfat milk powder

1½ tbsp sugar

scant 1 tsp fast-acting yeast

1 tsp baking powder

pinch of sea salt

6 tbsp warm water

1 tbsp vegetable oil, plus more for brushing

1 handful of cilantro

1 lime, quartered

1 small cucumber, cut into thin rounds

4 green onions, thinly sliced on the diagonal

Whisk together the soy sauce, mirin, honey, and chile in a shallow baking dish. Add the salmon fillets, turning once to coat. Cover and place in the refrigerator.

To make the bun dough: Put the dry ingredients into a large bowl. Mix together, then make a well in the center and add the wet ingredients. Use a spoon to bring everything together, then turn out and knead for 2 to 3 minutes, or until you have a smooth dough. Place the dough in an oiled bowl and cover with a kitchen towel or a piece of plastic wrap. Set aside to rise for 45 minutes, or until nearly doubled in size.

Cut out 8 pieces of parchment paper about 4 by 4 in. Dust the work surface and your hands with flour. Roll the dough into a fat sausage and cut it into eight equal parts. Roll each piece into a ball, then dust your work surface again, flatten a ball, and roll out with a rolling pin into a 2¾-by-6 in oval shape about ⅛ in thick. Brush lightly with oil and fold in half. Place each on a square of parchment paper and leave to rise for 30 minutes.

Preheat the oven to 400°F. Place the salmon in the oven and cook for 20 minutes, spooning the marinade over the fish about 10 minutes into the cooking time.

Set up a steamer and place the bun dough on the parchment paper directly into it. Do this in batches if you don't have lots of space for them all, as they expand as they cook. Steam for 5 to 8 minutes, or until fluffy, pale, and firm to the touch.

While you are steaming the buns, place the cilantro, lime, cucumber, and green onions in separate bowls. When the salmon is cooked, pour any remaining marinade into a small jug. Serve the steamed buns with the teriyaki salmon, the bowls of garnishes, and the sauce on the side for self-assembly.

Whole-wheat open lasagna with creamy spinach and poached egg

Serves	Preparation time:	Resting time:	Cooking time:
4 as a light dinner or lunch	10 minutes	30 minutes	15 to 20 minutes

Normally, I'm not one to make my own pasta, despite having bought a pasta machine many years ago on my first trip to Naples (which was so heavy I ended up paying extra baggage fees). Getting the machine out and having to deal with all the cleaning afterward has always deterred me. However, as I discovered when I was testing this recipe, making your own pasta doesn't have to be hard or time-consuming. And don't be put off by the idea of the whole-wheat flour. It's not traditional, but it works particularly well with the robust flavor of the spinach.

For the pasta dough

¾ cup plus 1 tbsp whole-wheat flour

½ tsp sea salt

½ tsp freshly grated nutmeg

1 egg

1 tbsp water

1 lb frozen spinach

salt and freshly ground pepper

2 tbsp crème fraîche

4 eggs

½ cup grated Parmesan cheese or another flavorsome hard cheese

To make the pasta dough: Mix together the flour, salt, and nutmeg in a large bowl. Crack in the egg and add the water. Bring together with a spoon, then turn out onto a floured work surface and knead into a smooth ball. Wrap in plastic wrap and chill in the refrigerator for 30 minutes.

Place the frozen spinach in a medium saucepan. Cover and cook over medium heat for 5 minutes, then uncover. Cook for 10 minutes more, until all the excess liquid has evaporated, stirring occasionally. Taste and season generously with salt and pepper, then stir in the crème fraîche.

Meanwhile, dust your work surface with flour, cut the dough into four parts, and roll each with a rolling pin into a very thin rectangle (about 5 by 8 in and 1/32 in thick).

Bring a medium saucepan of salted water to a gentle simmer and a large saucepan of salted water to a boil. Crack 1 egg into a ramekin (I find this makes it easiest to guide them into the water), then stir the water in the medium pan, making a little whirlpool, and pour the egg into the center. Repeat with the rest of the eggs and let cook for 2 to 3 minutes. Using a slotted spoon, remove the eggs from the water and drain on a clean paper towel. At this point, you can cut off any stray bits of white if you want to tidy them up.

Plunge the pasta sheets into the large pan of boiling water for 2 to 3 minutes, then remove with a slotted spoon and divide among shallow bowls. Add a dollop of the spinach, follow with an egg, then fold the top of the sheet back over to encase the egg. Sprinkle with plenty of Parmesan cheese and serve.

Cherry—glazed lamb shanks with pilaf

Serves
4

Preparation time:
20 minutes

Cooking time:
3 hours

Shanks seem to be the choice cut of lamb in gastropubs and restaurants. More affordable than shoulder and perfect for slow cooking, they require minimum effort for maximum flavor. Lamb can be a bit of a flavor bully, dominating a dish, so you need some distinct flavors to stand up to it. The cherries and red wine in this dish form fruity notes that really mellow out the lamb. There's not much to making it—browning the meat, popping the ingredients in, and letting the magic happen in the pot.

3 tbsp all-purpose flour

sea salt and freshly ground pepper

14 oz lamb shanks

1 to 2 tbsp olive oil

1⅔ cups red wine such as Pinot Noir or Beaujolais

2½ cups chicken stock

two 15-oz pitted cherries, drained

1½ cups basmati rice

¼ cup butter

1 onion, peeled and finely chopped

½ cup pistachios, coarsely chopped

2 stalks celery, finely chopped

1 large carrot, peeled and finely chopped

2 tsp cornstarch

2 tbsp water

1 handful of finely chopped fresh parsley

zest of 1 unwaxed lemon

Preheat the oven to 325°F. Mix the flour, 1 tsp salt, and 1 tsp pepper in a large bowl and add the lamb shanks, dusting each one well with the flour. Pour the oil into a large lidded ovenproof casserole pan over medium heat and brown the shanks in batches. Pour in the wine, stock, and one can of the cherries. Bring everything to a boil, cover, and braise in the oven for 2 hours, or until the meat feels very tender when poked with a knife. Remove the lid and cook for 30 minutes longer.

While the lamb is cooking, rinse the rice in water, drain, then repeat three times. Cook the rice in a large pan of boiling salted water for 5 minutes and drain well. Meanwhile, melt the butter in a large lidded nonstick frying pan over medium-low heat. Add the onion, pistachios, celery, and carrot and fry gently for 10 to 15 minutes, or until they soften, then stir in the par-cooked rice and season with salt. Wrap the lid of the pan in a clean kitchen towel and place on top (the towel will absorb moisture so the rice stays crispy). Cook for 25 minutes over very low heat—you want the rice to crisp up on the base of the pan.

Put the cornstarch and water into a small bowl and mix to a smooth paste. Transfer the lamb shanks to a plate and wrap in aluminum foil to keep warm. Pour the sauce through a sieve into a jug to strain out the cherries (reserve them for later). Pour the sauce into a large pan, then skim off the fat with a large spoon and whisk in the diluted cornstarch. Bring to a simmer and continue whisking for 10 to 15 minutes, or until the sauce coats the back of the spoon and becomes glossy. Season with plenty of pepper, and salt if needed. Return the reserved braised cherries to the sauce, along with the second can of cherries, and warm through.

Fluff up the rice pilaf with a fork and toss in the parsley and lemon zest. Divide among plates, placing a shank on each plate and pouring over some cherry sauce and cherries before serving.

Pistachio and
pomegranate cake

Sweets

Chocolate
fancies

Shake-and-make
ice cream

I've always had a keen interest in getting to the roots of an idea. To discover that the word "dessert" originates from the French was no surprise, but its etymology was not what I expected. Its linguistic roots come from the mid-sixteenth-century word *desservir*, which means "to clear away a table." Back in medieval times, both savory and sweet dishes would share the table simultaneously, and the serving of a dessert at the end of the meal was not de rigueur until a couple of centuries later. However, I can't think of a better way of finishing a meal than on a sweet note, leaving your guests on a sugar high.

Desserts are in my blood. From my fond childhood memories of licking cake batter off spoons, making gingerbread with my mum, or sitting at my Austrian grandma's table and watching her stretch out strudel dough to perfecting a buttery *pain au chocolat* in Paris, I feel at home when I'm whisking, folding, whipping, or piping. There's something very soothing and satisfying about delicately smoothing icing onto a cake with strokes of your spatula, or placing that last cherry on a dessert to complete a dish. The skill and craftsmanship are what initially drew me to study patisserie in Paris; unlike other sorts of cooking, there is a certain scientific precision to desserts. Too much butter and the batter spreads; too hot and the cake cracks—but don't let that put you off. It's very reassuring to know that if you measure your ingredients and follow the method in the recipe, all will go well. And then there's the great pleasure in bringing the dessert to life with the decoration—like the marbling on my Pistachio and Pomegranate Cake (page 163), or the Jackson Pollock–esque chocolate "dribble" on my Chocolate and Zucchini Fondant Fancies (page 196).

But it's not just about the eye candy, it has to taste good too! Whether it's combining classic flavors such as cherry and chocolate in the Black Forest Gâteau Bowls (page 179), or unusual ones like those in my Mini Orange Trifles with Candied Carrots (page 160), or different textures, such as the crunchy and creamy elements in the Edible Forest Floor (page 159), the recipes in this chapter will surprise, excite, and tickle your taste buds.

Berry tartlets with cream cheese filling

Makes	Preparation time:	Baking time:	Cooling time:
6	30 minutes	35 minutes	20 minutes

These delightful tartlets are easy to make, and look impressive with a little bouquet of fresh berries perched on top.

2 to 3 tbsp granulated sugar

6 oz puff pastry

6 tbsp unsalted butter, at room temperature

1 cup confectioners' sugar, plus more for dusting

6 tbsp full-fat cream cheese, at room temperature

5 to 7 oz fresh berries (strawberries, raspberries, blueberries), washed

Preheat the oven to 350°F.

Dust your work surface with half the granulated sugar and roll out the pastry into a rectangle, roughly 6 by 8 in. Dust with the remaining sugar and roll the rolling pin over it to press in the sugar. Tightly roll it up, starting from the horizontal side closest to you. Cut the roll into six equal-size pieces, roughly 1¼ in wide. Take one piece and place it spiral-side up in a muffin pan. Use your thumb to push the dough outward, evenly lining the base and sides of the pan. Repeat with the rest of the spirals.

Prick the base of each one with a fork, then line with small rounds of parchment paper and add ceramic baking weights to each. Bake for 20 minutes, then remove the weights and parchment and return to the oven for 10 to 15 minutes, or until lightly golden and cooked through (check by lifting one out of the pan). Remove from the pan immediately (otherwise they will caramelize and stick), and set aside to cool on a wire rack.

While the tartlet bases are baking, using an electric hand mixer, beat together the butter and confectioners' sugar for 2 minutes, or until light and fluffy. Beat in the cream cheese until well blended.

Put a dollop of filling on each of the tartlet bases. Decorate the tops with berries and dust with confectioners' sugar, if you like, before serving.

Get ahead
Once cooled, the baked tartlet bases can be kept in an airtight container for up to 5 days. They also freeze well.

Tip
Don't refrigerate the ganache or the chocolate yogurt as they will become too hard to use.

Get ahead
The meringue mushrooms without ganache will keep for about 1 week in an airtight container.

Edible forest floor

Serves	Preparation time:	Cooking time:	Cooling time:
4	30 minutes	1½ to 2 hours	2 hours minimum

The Swedish forest inspired this dessert. I've spent many summers in Sweden picking berries. Plated desserts can look intimidating to the home cook, but it's simply a case of bringing together different tastes, textures, and sometimes temperatures to work in harmony. Here you get crunch from the meringue, richness from the ganache, creaminess from the yogurt, and tartness from the berries. It's the combination of these elements that makes the dessert work.

For the meringue mushrooms

1 egg white

pinch of sea salt

¼ cup granulated sugar

For the dark chocolate ganache

3½ oz dark chocolate (70% cacao), broken into pieces

6 tbsp heavy cream

pinch of sea salt

For the milk chocolate yogurt

5¾ oz milk chocolate, broken into pieces

¾ cup plus 2 tbsp natural full-fat yogurt

4 chocolate wafer cookies

1 tbsp cocoa powder

4 oz blueberries or berries of your choice

fresh mint leaves

To make the meringue mushrooms: Preheat the oven to 200°F. Line a baking sheet with parchment paper. Combine the egg white and salt in a large glass bowl and beat with an electric hand mixer. When really frothy, gradually add the sugar, whisking until the meringue is thick and glossy and forms stiff, shiny peaks.

Spoon the meringue into a piping bag fitted with a ⅜-in tip, and squeeze out into 12 round 1-in mounds to make the mushroom caps on the prepared baking sheet. To make each stem, separately squeeze out a bit of meringue onto the baking sheet while pulling the bag straight up so each stem stands 1½ in high. Dip your finger in water and smooth the top of the mushroom caps so that they're rounded. Bake in the center of the oven for 1½ hours, then turn off the oven. Leave them for 2 hours or as long as overnight, until completely cool and dry.

To make the dark chocolate ganache: Place the chocolate in a heatproof bowl. Put the cream and salt into a small saucepan and bring to a simmer, then pour over the chocolate. Let sit for 2 minutes, then stir until thoroughly incorporated. Let cool for about 30 minutes, or until room temperature, then spoon into a piping bag fitted with a ⅛-in tip.

To make the milk chocolate yogurt: Place the chocolate and yogurt in a heatproof bowl over a pan of just-simmering water (don't let the bowl touch the water). Stir until the chocolate has melted, using a whisk to mix well.

Use a chopstick to make a small hole in the underside of each mushroom cap. Pipe a small amount of chocolate ganache into each hole, then stick the stems in.

Spread a layer of chocolate yogurt on each dessert plate. Crumble in the chocolate cookies and pipe on teardrops of the ganache. Stick a few mushrooms into the yogurt, dust with cocoa powder, and then sprinkle the berries and mint leaves over, dividing them equally among the plates, before serving.

Mini orange trifles with candied carrot

Serves	Preparation time:	Cooking time:	Chilling time:
4	30 minutes	15 minutes	4 hours minimum

This recipe takes its inspiration from the classic Provençal dish *petits farcis*, in which Mediterranean vegetables are stuffed with rice or ground meat. I decided to go a bit retro, filling oranges with gelatin, but adding candied carrots and snow-white meringue to transform a children's classic into something a bit more modern.

For the candied carrots

¾ cup granulated sugar

10 tbsp water

1 large carrot, peeled and julienned

2 large oranges

2 leaves of gelatin

For the meringue topping

½ cup plus 2 tsp granulated sugar

2 egg whites

To make the candied carrots: Place the sugar, water, and carrot in a large saucepan over gentle heat. Bring to a boil, stirring occasionally until the sugar has dissolved , then simmer briskly for 10 minutes, or until the carrot looks shiny. Drain in a sieve set over a bowl.

Halve the oranges and juice them carefully (maintain their shape as they will act as the gelatin containers). Strain the juice through a sieve and set aside. Use a teaspoon to scoop the inside membrane out of the orange halves, until you are left with just a thin layer of pith and the skin. Cut a slice off the bottom of each orange half so they sit upright.

Soak the gelatin in a bowl of cold water for 5 minutes. Mix the carrot syrup with the orange juice in a small saucepan and heat very gently until warm, then squeeze out the soaked gelatin and stir into the liquid until dissolved. Pour into a jug.

Mold some aluminum foil around the bases of the orange halves to help them sit straight. Place on a baking sheet and transfer to the refrigerator. Pour the orange gelatin into the molds while they're on the refrigerator shelf. Divide some of the candied carrots between the orange halves. Let set in the refrigerator for at least 4 hours, or up to overnight.

To make the meringue topping: Spread out the sugar on a baking sheet and place in the oven for about 10 minutes. Whisk the egg whites until frothy, and add the hot sugar 1 tbsp at a time. Continue to whisk until cool and glossy. Place the meringue in a piping bag.

Pipe a large dollop of meringue on top of each orange half. If you like, use a broiler or blow torch to lightly toast the tips of the meringue. Decorate with a few strips of the candied carrot, and serve.

Tip

Use any leftover candied carrot to decorate a carrot cake. The candied carrots keep well in the refrigerator for a few days.

Get ahead

The gelatin will keep in the refrigerator for a couple of days, but make the meringue just before serving.

Pistachio and pomegranate cake

Serves	Preparation time:	Baking time:
8 to 10	20 minutes	50 minutes

Turkish pastries, such as the intensely sweet and extremely sticky baklava, were nothing new to me; however, the pomegranate juice stands that cropped up on Istanbul's street corners were a delightful discovery. The dark red juice makes for a refreshing drink, and although it's a nightmare if you get it on your clothes, it's perfect for coloring icing the natural way.

For the cake

1 cup shelled pistachios

¾ cup granulated sugar

⅔ cup sunflower oil

2 eggs, lightly beaten

1 tsp vanilla extract

1½ cups natural yogurt

2½ cups all-purpose flour

2 tsp baking powder

½ tsp sea salt

½ pomegranate

For the yogurt icing

2 cups confectioners' sugar

3½ tbsp natural yogurt

To make the cake: Preheat the oven to 325°F. Butter and flour an 8-in springform pan.

Using a food processor, grind the pistachios to a fine powder.

Combine the granulated sugar and oil in the bowl of a stand mixer fitted with the paddle attachment and mix for 2 minutes, until the sugar has dissolved. Gradually add the eggs and vanilla. Fold in the yogurt. Gently fold in the flour, baking powder, salt, and ground pistachios. Spoon the batter into the prepared pan.

Bake for 50 minutes, or until a skewer comes out clean. Let cool for 5 minutes, then release the sides of the pan and invert the cake onto a wire rack to cool, lifting away the bottom of the pan.

When the cake is cool, hold the pomegranate skin-side up in a bowl with your fingers spread out. Hit the outside of the skin with a wooden spoon. The seeds and juice will fall through the gaps between your fingers into the bowl.

To make the yogurt icing: Sift the confectioners' sugar into a bowl, then add the yogurt and mix well to get a thick pouring consistency.

Pour the icing on top of the cooled cake, gently guiding it down the sides. Once the icing has stopped dripping, take the pomegranate juice and dot several drops along the top of the cake. Drag a skewer or toothpick in a figure-eight pattern through the drips of pomegranate, swirling it all around the cake.

Stick the pomegranate seeds to the side of the cake when the icing has stopped dripping. (If it's difficult to make them stick, chill the cake for 10 minutes in the refrigerator first.) Slice and serve.

Underground éclairs

Makes 8	Preparation time: 35 minutes	Cooking time: 25 to 30 minutes	Cooling time: 1 hour

These tubes of choux pastry are my ode to London's almighty Tube. Instead of opting for artificial food colorings, I've picked some fresh fruits that correspond with the colors of some of my favorite Underground lines. Well, no one actually likes the District line, let's be honest, but kiwis accessorize these éclairs beautifully.

For the choux pastry

¼ cup water

¼ cup whole milk

¼ cup unsalted butter, cubed

½ tsp sea salt

½ tsp granulated sugar

⅔ cup all-purpose flour

2 eggs

For the pastry cream

3 egg yolks

1 tbsp plus 1 tsp granulated sugar

2 tbsp cornstarch

1 cup whole milk

1 vanilla bean

For the icing

⅔ cup plus 2 tbsp confectioners' sugar, sifted

½ egg white

¾ to 1 tsp lemon juice

To make the choux pastry: Preheat the oven to 350°F.

Pour the water and milk into a medium saucepan and add the butter, salt, and granulated sugar. Place the pan over high heat and melt the butter. Bring to a boil, then turn the heat to low and stir in the flour. Beat hard. At this point the mixture will have the consistency of lumpy mashed potatoes. Continue beating for about 1 minute, until you have a smooth ball that pulls away from the sides of the pan without sticking.

Take the pan off the heat and continue to beat for 4 to 5 minutes, or until the dough is cold enough to touch. Mix in the eggs one at a time—the dough will go lumpy when you add them, but beating continuously will smooth it out. Once both eggs are incorporated and the mixture is smooth, put the dough into a piping bag fitted with a ¾-in plain tip.

Line a large baking sheet with parchment paper, dotting a little dough in each corner to stick down the paper. Pipe a 4-in line of the dough at a 45-degree angle. Repeat with the remaining dough to make 8 éclairs. Bake for 25 minutes, or until golden and crisp. Let cool on a wire rack.

To make the pastry cream: Put the egg yolks and granulated sugar in a large bowl and whisk until light and fluffy. Whisk in the cornstarch. Pour the milk into a saucepan over medium-high heat. Split the vanilla bean lengthwise, scrape out the seeds, and add them to the milk. Heat the milk until bubbles form around the edge and wisps of steam rise from the center, then remove from the heat.

Pour the milk in a slow stream into the egg mixture, whisking vigorously. Transfer the mixture to a clean saucepan and whisk continuously over medium heat. Make sure you scrape the sides

5 small strawberries, hulled

1 kiwi fruit, peeled

2 slices pineapple, peeled

2 oz raspberries

and the bottom to prevent it from burning. The cream will start to thicken. Once it releases a bubble or two, take it off the heat. Pour into a bowl and place plastic wrap directly on the surface so that it doesn't form a skin. Let cool to room temperature, then refrigerate for at least 1 hour before using.

When ready to use, beat the pastry cream to smooth it out and transfer to a piping bag. Halve the éclairs horizontally and pipe pastry cream inside, then put the tops back on.

To make the icing: Mix the confectioners' sugar with the egg white and lemon juice until you have a very thick paste. (If it's too runny it won't stick to the fruits properly, in which case just add more confectioners' sugar, 1 tsp at a time.)

Thinly slice the strawberries, kiwi fruit, and pineapple. Spread a thin line of icing along the top of each éclair lid. Decorate two éclairs with the strawberries (for the Central Line), lining them up along the top of the pastry and using the icing to stick them down. Then decorate the rest of the éclairs with the kiwi fruits (for the District Line), pineapple (for the Circle Line), and raspberries (for the Hammersmith & City Line). Serve immediately.

Spiced apple tray cake

Serves
14

Preparation time:
20 minutes

Cooking time:
50 to 60 minutes

There's nothing more homey than the smell of cinnamon and baking apples. This would be the perfect cake to bake if you were trying to sell your home.

I had an amazing slice of apple cake when I was in Amsterdam, where they pride themselves on its buttery caramel pastry with its mix of soft tender apple pieces and ones with bite (a combination of apples is a must). I've added ground toasted hazelnuts to my batter, which gives the finished product a deliciously nutty, almost frangipane flavor. The pastry is similar to one used in the Austrian cake my mum and aunts make, *Linzertorte* (hazelnut pastry with raspberry jam)—one of my favorites.

2 cups blanched hazelnuts or almonds

1½ cups plus 2 tbsp unsalted butter, at room temperature

1 cup plus 2 tbsp firmly packed light brown sugar

a good pinch of sea salt

3 eggs, lightly beaten

3¼ cups all-purpose flour

4 tsp baking powder

For the filling

2 tbsp firmly packed light brown sugar

1 tbsp ground cinnamon

½ tsp ground ginger

¼ tsp grated nutmeg

2 tbsp cornstarch

3 firm apples, such as Braeburn, Royal Gala, or Cox

5 cooking apples, such as Golden Delicious

1 tbsp confectioners' sugar

whipped cream or vanilla ice cream for serving

Preheat the oven to 325°F. Butter a 12-in square cake pan.

Put the nuts in a dry frying pan over medium heat. Toast for about 5 minutes, or until the nuts are golden, stirring frequently. Remove from the pan and let the nuts cool completely, then grind them in a food processor to a fine powder.

Cream together the butter, brown sugar, and salt in a large bowl. Gradually mix in the eggs. In a separate bowl, mix together the flour, baking powder, and ground nuts, then gently fold into the creamed butter.

Spread two-thirds of the batter across the base of the prepared pan. Keep the base even, but scrape it up a little at the sides to create an edge to hold the filling.

To make the filling: Mix the brown sugar, spices, and cornstarch in a large bowl. Peel, core, and cut the apples into ¾-in cubes, then toss well in the spice mix.

Scatter the filling over the cake batter and level out evenly. Place the remaining cake batter in a piping bag with the end snipped off, and pipe four lines of batter one way over the top of the cake, then four lines the other way, to make a lattice pattern.

Bake for 50 to 60 minutes, or until the crust is golden brown. Let cool for 10 minutes, then cut into pieces and dust with the confectioners' sugar. Serve warm with a dollop of whipped cream or a scoop of vanilla ice cream.

Tip

If you can't find blanched hazelnuts, toast unblanched ones for 8 to 10 minutes at 250°F and rub the skins off with a clean kitchen towel.

Raspberry and grape brioche and butter pudding

Serves	Preparation time:	Baking time:
4	20 minutes	15 minutes

In the sweet department, France is best known for its extravagant patisseries. However, when you head out to the countryside, heartier portions and rustic-looking cakes are more the norm. This is where the French *grand-mère* is the queen of the kitchen, not some Parisian chef with lots of airs and graces.

Bread and butter pudding isn't exactly on the menu in France, but the brioche, fruity compote, and crème anglaise give this British classic a fantastic French twist.

For the compote

2 tbsp sugar

10½ oz frozen raspberries

4 tbsp Chambord or other raspberry-flavored liqueur

10½ oz dark red grapes (preferably muscat), halved and seeded

For the crème anglaise

1 cup whole milk

1 cup heavy cream

1 vanilla bean

4 egg yolks

¼ cup granulated sugar

¼ cup granulated sugar

eight ½-in-thick slices day-old brioche

2 knobs of soft unsalted butter (optional)

To make the compote: Place the sugar, raspberries, and Chambord in a medium saucepan over low heat. Cover and cook, stirring occasionally, for about 6 minutes, or until the raspberries have softened. Remove from the heat and stir in the grape halves, then cover the pan and set aside.

To make the crème anglaise: Pour the milk and cream into a medium saucepan. Split the vanilla bean lengthwise and scrape out the seeds into the pan, adding the pod too. Bring to a simmer over medium-low heat. In a separate large bowl, whisk the egg yolks with the sugar. Pour a little of the hot cream mixture into the yolks while whisking vigorously, then gradually pour in the rest of the liquid. Remove the vanilla pod and transfer the mixture to a clean pan.

Over medium-low heat, whisk the cream-egg mixture continuously until it thickens to the consistency of heavy whipping cream; don't let it come close to the boiling point or it might separate. As soon as it has thickened, pour it straight into a pitcher or bowl and cover the surface with plastic wrap to prevent a skin from forming. Set aside until ready to use.

Preheat the broiler. Line a baking sheet with aluminum foil. Spread the sugar on a large plate. If the brioche is fresh, simply dip it in the sugar; otherwise, spread butter on both sides of the slices before pressing into the sugar. Place on the prepared baking sheet. Broil, turning over after a couple of minutes or when the brioche is golden. (Beware, it can brown very quickly.)

Reheat the compote and the crème anglaise over low heat until warmed through. Place a slice of brioche in each of four shallow bowls. Pour on 2 to 3 tbsp of the hot compote and top with another slice of brioche. Ladle over the warm crème anglaise, followed by several more spoonfuls of the compote, and serve immediately.

Plum gelatin with elderflower chantilly

Serves	Preparation time:	Cooking time:	Resting time:
12	30 minutes	20 minutes	12 hours minimum

I love the wibble-wobble of gelatin on a plate. The texture is immensely satisfying when paired with lashings of chantilly cream, proving that gelatin isn't just fun for kids.

For the plum gelatin

4½ lb purple or red plums

3 cups plus 2 tbsp water

3¼ cups granulated sugar

12 gelatin leaves

For the crystallized basil leaves

1 egg white

4 to 6 tbsp granulated sugar

1 handful of basil leaves

For the chantilly cream

2 cups plus 1 tbsp heavy cream

⅓ cup plus 1 tbsp granulated sugar

3 tbsp elderflower cordial

To make the plum gelatin: Halve the plums, leaving the pits in, and place in a large saucepan with the water and sugar. Bring to a simmer over medium heat, stirring frequently to help dissolve the sugar, then lower the heat. Simmer the plums, uncovered, for 15 to 20 minutes, or until mushy.

Fill a large, wide container halfway with cold water, then add the gelatin leaves one at a time, so they don't stick together. Let soak for 10 minutes.

Drain the plums in a colander set over a large bowl, reserving the syrup. Then pass the plums through a fine sieve into the bowl, pressing out as much of the plum juice as you can. Discard the pits, but keep the stewed fruit for another day (see Tip).

Squeeze the water from the soaked gelatin and add to the plum syrup. Stir until dissolved, then pour into your gelatin mold. Dab with a paper towel to remove any scum on the surface. Let cool completely, then cover and refrigerate for at least 12 hours.

To make the crystallized basil leaves: Place the egg white in a bowl and whisk lightly to loosen. Place the sugar on a plate, and have a clean plate at hand. Dip a clean paintbrush or pastry brush into the egg white and delicately coat a basil leaf. Sprinkle the leaf with sugar, then place on the clean plate. Repeat with the remaining leaves and set aside in a cool, dark place.

To make the chantilly cream: Before serving, whip the cream with the sugar until soft peaks form, then fold in the elderflower cordial.

Remove the plum gelatin from its mold and place on a cake stand. Dollop the chantilly cream around the top of the gelatin and crown with the basil leaves before serving.

Tips

The leftover stewed fruit goes well with yogurt and granola.

Use the basil leaves within 1 to 2 hours of making, as they tend to lose their vibrant color.

Honey-roasted peach crema catalana

Makes	Preparation time:	Cooking time:	Standing time:
4	20 minutes	45 minutes	30 minutes infusing, plus 2 hours chilling

One of the best parts of a *crema catalana* is breaking through the caramel crust and diving into the rich, smooth cream, but I often find it overbearingly sweet. So here I have swapped the caramel topping for peaches (nectarines or apricots would work too), which I spotted in all the markets when I visited the Costa Brava. Placed on top of the creams, the juicy, honey-roasted peaches create a delicious fruity crust.

Vanilla bean is normally used to flavor the cream, but I like to use the kernels from inside the peach pits, which add a subtle almond flavor. It can be a pain to crack them open, though, so if you want to cheat and use a splash of almond extract, I will forgive you.

2 ripe peaches

3 tbsp runny honey

2 cups whole milk

4 egg yolks

⅓ cup granulated sugar

2 tbsp cornstarch

Preheat the oven to 325°F.

Halve the peaches and remove and reserve the pits. Place the peaches cut-side up on a baking sheet and drizzle with the honey. Cover with parchment paper and roast in the oven for 30 minutes, or until tender but not mushy.

Meanwhile, use a hammer or nutcracker to crack open the peach pits and remove the kernels. If using a hammer, place each pit in a clean kitchen towel, then fold the cloth over the top to secure the stone before bashing it. Place the kernels in a saucepan and add the milk. Slowly bring to a scalding point, then remove from the heat and set aside. Let infuse for 30 minutes.

In a large bowl, whisk the egg yolks with the sugar for 2 to 3 minutes until pale, then add the cornstarch. Slowly whisk in the cooled milk. Pour the custard into a clean saucepan and place over gentle heat, whisking continuously, for 8 to 10 minutes, or until the mixture has thickened and releases a bubble or two.

Remove and discard the kernels and divide the mixture between four ramekins. Peel the skins off the peach halves and place one half cut-side down on top of the custard in each ramekin. Leave to cool for 30 minutes, or until room temperature, then place in the refrigerator and let set for at least 2 hours before serving.

Tip

Crack your peach pits gently, so as not to break the kernels.

Black forest gâteau bowls

Makes
8 bowls

Preparation time:
45 minutes

Resting time:
30 minutes

Cooking time:
30 to 35 minutes

This recipe combines all the classic ingredients of the great retro Black Forest gâteau. For an impressive, dainty twist, try serving it in these cute homemade chocolate cups.

For the cake

¾ cup all-purpose flour

2 tbsp cocoa powder

1 tsp baking powder

½ cup plus 2 tbsp granulated sugar

2 eggs

¼ cup unsalted butter, melted

For the chocolate bowls

14 oz dark chocolate (70% cacao), broken into pieces

2 tbsp vegetable or sunflower oil

For the cherries

14 oz cherries

6 tbsp water

½ cup granulated sugar

1¼ cups heavy cream

1 tbsp confectioners' sugar, sifted

chocolate shavings for garnish

To make the cake: Preheat the oven to 325°F. Butter and flour a 12-in round cake pan.

Sift together the flour, cocoa powder, and baking powder in a bowl. In a separate large bowl or the bowl of a stand mixer, whisk the granulated sugar and eggs for 7 to 8 minutes, or until pale and fluffy. Add the melted butter and fold into the eggs, followed by the sifted flour mixture. Pour the batter into the prepared pan. Bake for 30 to 35 minutes, or until a skewer comes out clean. Remove from the pan after 5 minutes and set on a wire rack to cool.

To make the chocolate bowls: Inflate eight small balloons to a roughly 4-in diameter, then tie them. Put the chocolate into a small heatproof bowl with the oil and place over a small pan of just-simmering water (don't let the bowl touch the water). Let melt, stirring occasionally, then set aside for 10 to 15 minutes. As it stands it will thicken; you want it to be the consistency of heavy cream. Cover a plate with some lightly oiled plastic wrap, then dip a balloon into the chocolate and place on the plate. Repeat with the remaining seven balloons. Put them into the refrigerator to set.

To make the cherries: Pit the cherries (setting aside 8 whole ones with stems for the garnish). Pour the water and granulated sugar into a medium saucepan over medium heat and bring to a simmer. Add the pitted cherries and cook gently for 10 minutes, then remove from the heat and let cool to room temperature. Place the cherries in the refrigerator to chill.

Once the first layer of chocolate on the balloons has set, repeat with a second layer. (You will probably need to remelt the chocolate.) Return to the refrigerator. Once set, the balloons can be removed. Simply snip across the top of them and let the air out, then gently pull away the balloons to reveal the bowls.

Whisk the cream with the confectioners' sugar until soft peaks form. Place in a piping bag. Cut the cake into small chunks and divide among the chocolate bowls. Top with the cherries, drizzling over some of the syrup. Pipe a swirl of cream on top of each bowl and garnish with one of the reserved whole cherries. Sprinkle with chocolate shavings before serving.

Tips

Don't dip the balloons into very hot chocolate, as they will explode and make a big mess. It's also better to dip them into a small bowl of chocolate to give the chocolate layer more depth.

It's easier to whip cream when the cream is really cold. If it's hot in your kitchen, place your bowl in the freezer before you whip.

Lemon lava cakes

Makes
6

Preparation time:
25 minutes

Cooking time:
30 minutes

Cooling time:
20 to 30 minutes

What do you get when you cross an Amalfi lemon, Vesuvius, and a cake? A lemon lava cake! Okay, I know my joke is appalling, but that's how I got the idea for this recipe. The Amalfi Coast is blessed with an abundance of citrus fruit trees, which line the coastal roads that cling to the cliffs. This little cake erupts like the nearby Mount Vesuvius, with a zingy hot lemon curd. It's dessert with attitude.

For the lemon curd
juice of 3 lemons

1 cup granulated sugar

2 eggs

pinch of sea salt

¼ cup cold unsalted butter, cubed

For the cake
½ cup unsalted butter, at room temperature

7 tbsp granulated sugar

2 eggs

2 tbsp whole milk

zest of 3 unwaxed lemons

¾ cup all-purpose flour

To make the lemon curd: Place the lemon juice, sugar, eggs, and salt in a medium saucepan over gentle heat and whisk continuously for 5 to 8 minutes, or until the mixture thickens. Whisk in the butter, cube by cube. Remove from the heat once all the butter has melted. Pour into a wide bowl and let cool for 20 to 30 minutes, or until room temperature. Pour into a heavy-duty resealable plastic bag and refrigerate until ready to use.

To make the cake: Preheat the oven to 350°F. Butter the ramekins and dust with 1 tbsp of the sugar.

Beat the butter and remaining 6 tbsp sugar until fluffy. Lightly beat the eggs and gradually add them to the mix, beating continuously, followed by the milk and lemon zest. Sift the flour into the mix and incorporate well. Divide the batter among the prepared ramekins, filling each just over half full.

Snip off the corner of the plastic bag holding the curd. Insert the tip into the center of each batter-filled ramekin. Pipe the curd into each one until the ramekins are two-thirds full. Place on a rimmed baking sheet.

Bake for 15 to 20 minutes, or until the tops are golden and spring back when touched.

Immediately run a knife around the edges of the cakes before turning them out of the ramekins and onto serving plates. Serve right away.

Tips
Make sure not to let the curd boil, as this will make it separate and give it an eggy taste.

The leftover lemon curd is delicious swirled into yogurt.

Get ahead
You can bake these straight from the freezer. Simply fill the ramekins as directed, wrap tightly, and place in the freezer for up to 1 month. Bake for about 25 minutes at 325°F.

BEAUTIFUL PASTRIES
SPOTTED IN ✖ A PÂTISSERIE

CRAZY CAKE DISPLAY IN A
RESTAURANT IN WARSAW

CUTE COFFEE ART IN
STOCKHOLM

TESTING RHUBARB AND
CUSTARD MILLEFEUILLE
✖ RECIPE

LOADS OF SPOONS AT
THE GRAND BAZAAR
IN ✖ ISTANBUL

STRAWBERRY CREAM
CAKE - YUM ! ✖

CHECKING OUT A NEW
PÂTISSERIE ✖ IN PARIS

COLORFUL SELECTION
OF ICE LOLLIES
IN NEW ✖ YORK CITY

RHUBARB WITH
HOMEMADE SPICED JUNKET
✖

FRESH FRUIT

coconut
chocolate
coffee

JAM

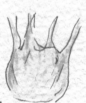

SUGAR

COPPER
POT

Lingonberry and raspberry Mazarin tart

Serves 10	Preparation time: 25 minutes	Baking time: 55 minutes	Chilling time: 30 minutes minimum

Small versions of this tart can be found in almost every bakery across Sweden. Traditionally filled with a dense almond paste and encased in a buttery crust, they are perfect with a cup of coffee for what the Swedes call *fika* (coffee and cake time). My variation has some fruity extras, with a lingonberry jam base and raspberries on top: a Swedish-style Bakewell tart fit to grace any Parisian patisserie.

For the pastry

¾ cup all-purpose flour

pinch of sea salt

1 tsp granulated sugar

¼ cup cold unsalted butter, cubed

1 egg yolk

1 tsp vodka, unflavored schnapps, or eau de vie

For the filling

5¼ oz blanched almonds

¼ cup granulated sugar

6 tbsp unsalted butter, at room temperature

½ tsp almond extract

pinch of sea salt

2 eggs

1 tbsp all-purpose flour

¾ cup lingonberry jam

½ cup confectioners' sugar

1 tbsp water

7 oz raspberries

To make the pastry: Mix together the flour, salt, and granulated sugar. Add the butter and rub together until you have a sandy texture. Combine the egg yolk and vodka and add to the mixture. Bring the mixture together, lightly kneading just until it is a smooth dough. Try not to overwork it.

Roll the pastry out into a 12-in circle between two sheets of parchment paper. Butter and flour a 12-in tart pan. Line the pan with the pastry, making sure the sides of the pastry are 1/16 in higher than the sides of the tart pan; trim away any excess pastry. Let rest in the refrigerator for at least 30 minutes, or up to overnight.

Preheat the oven to 325°F. Line the pastry with parchment paper and fill with ceramic baking weights. Place the tart pan on a baking sheet and bake for 20 minutes, then remove the paper and weights and bake for 10 minutes more. Remove from the oven and set aside to cool. Leave the oven on.

To make the filling: Toast the blanched almonds in a dry frying pan, stirring continuously, for 3 to 4 minutes, or until golden. Tip out onto a plate and let cool, then blend with the granulated sugar in a food processor until fine. Add the butter, almond extract, and salt and pulse to combine. Add the eggs and flour and pulse briefly again to combine.

Spread the jam on the base of the tart. Transfer the almond paste into a piping bag and pipe it in a spiral, starting from the center and moving outward. Return the tart to the oven to bake for 20 minutes, or until the filling is firm and lightly golden. Let cool.

Mix the confectioners' sugar with the water to make a very thick paste. Spread over the tart and arrange the raspberries on top. Cut into wedges and serve.

Rhubarb and custard millefeuilles

Makes
4

Preparation time:
40 minutes

Cooking time:
35 minutes

Resting time:
1 to 2 hours

Rhubarb and custard is a classic combination I remember fondly from my childhood, when I would be given the hard-boiled flavored sweets on long car journeys to keep me quiet. My dessert version has kept a few of my dinner guests quiet too.

For the custard

3 egg yolks

Scant 3 tbsp granulated sugar

2 tbsp cornstarch

1 cup whole milk

½ vanilla bean

For the pastry

one 14-oz package ready-rolled puff pastry, removed from the refrigerator 20 minutes before using

1 egg, beaten

2 tbsp granulated sugar

For the rhubarb compote

14 oz pink rhubarb, washed, trimmed, and cut into 4-in pieces

¼ cup granulated sugar

1 tbsp confectioners' sugar

To make the custard: Whisk the egg yolks with the granulated sugar for 2 to 3 minutes, or until light and thick, then whisk in the cornstarch. Pour the milk into a saucepan, split the vanilla bean lengthwise, scrape out the seeds, and add them to the milk along with the pod. Bring the milk to a boil and turn off the heat. Pour the milk in a slow stream into the egg mixture, whisking vigorously.

Transfer the mixture to a clean saucepan and whisk continuously over medium heat. (Make sure you scrape the sides and the bottom; otherwise, it will burn.) The cream will start to thicken. Once it releases a bubble or two, remove it from the heat. Pour the custard into a wide bowl and set aside to cool to room temperature. Transfer to a large piping bag fitted with a ⅜-in tip and place in a pitcher so it stays upright. Chill in the refrigerator for 1 to 2 hours.

To make the pastry: Preheat the oven to 350°F. Line a baking sheet with parchment paper.

Cut the puff pastry into 12 rectangles, measuring 1½ by 4 in, and place on the prepared baking sheet. Brush lightly with the beaten egg and sprinkle with the granulated sugar. Cover the glazed rectangles with parchment paper, then place another baking sheet on top; this will stop the pastry from rising as it bakes. Bake for 30 minutes.

To make the rhubarb compote: Toss the rhubarb in the granulated sugar and place in a small baking dish or roasting pan in the oven, on a rack under the pastry, for 20 minutes. The rhubarb should be tender but not mushy.

Pipe two blobs of custard onto an individual serving plate. Stick a pastry rectangle on top, then place three or four rhubarb pieces on the pastry. Gently place another pastry rectangle over the rhubarb. Pipe two lines of custard on the second rectangle and top with a third rectangle. Repeat to make four millefeuilles. Dust with the confectioners' sugar and serve immediately.

Tip

If your pastry rectangles don't look quite done after 30 minutes, remove from the oven and take off the top baking sheet and paper. Place the pastries back in the oven for 6 to 8 minutes longer.

Strawberry and cream layer cake

Makes 1 cake	Preparation time: 40 minutes	Cooking time: 45 to 50 minutes

Strawberries and cream are a match made in heaven. Combine that with the sound of Wimbledon on the TV and you pretty much have my memories of British summers.

For the spiced strawberries

1¾ lb strawberries, halved

10 tbsp water

¾ cup granulated sugar

pinch of sea salt

1 tsp freshly ground pepper

For the cake

3 eggs

½ cup plus 2 tbsp granulated sugar

6 tbsp unsalted butter, melted

½ cup plus 3 tbsp natural yogurt

2½ cups all-purpose flour

1 tbsp baking powder

pinch of sea salt

For the whipped cream

1 vanilla bean, halved and seeds scraped out

3 cups plus 2 tbsp heavy cream

½ cup granulated sugar

To make the spiced strawberries: Reserve six berries for garnishing. Place the strawberries, water, sugar, salt, and pepper in a medium saucepan and bring to a boil over medium heat. Stir until the sugar has completely dissolved. Remove from the heat, let cool to room temperature, and chill in the refrigerator until needed.

To make the cake: Preheat the oven to 325°F. Butter an 8-in round cake pan and line it with parchment paper. Put the eggs and sugar into the bowl of a stand mixer fitted with the whisk attachment and whisk for about 5 minutes, or until thick, pale, and fluffy. Pour in the melted butter and yogurt.

Sift the flour, baking powder, and salt into a separate bowl and mix well. Gently fold into the egg mixture. Pour the batter into the prepared pan.

Bake for 45 to 50 minutes, or until a skewer comes out clean. Remove the pan from the oven and let rest for 5 minutes. Remove the cake from the pan and place on a wire rack. Let cool for at least 30 minutes.

Slice the cake horizontally into three layers. If you have a plate with a lip, you can do this by placing the whole cake upside down on the plate and using the edge of the plate to guide the bread knife across in a straight line, removing the peaked top (you can discard this). Repeat until you have three layers of cake.

To make the whipped cream: Add the vanilla seeds to the cream and whip with the sugar until firm enough to ice the cake.

Pour the spiced strawberries into a sieve set over a bowl and let drain thoroughly.

Invert the top cake layer as the base of the cake (the original flat base of the cake can be used as the top, giving a smooth finish). Use a pastry brush to dab the cut side of the cake generously with the syrup drained from the strawberries. Spread a quarter of the whipped cream on top of the cake, then add half of the spiced strawberries. Place another layer of cake over the berries and repeat the process. Finally, spread or pipe the rest of the cream around the sides and on top of the cake. Garnish the cake with the reserved strawberries. Store, covered, in the refrigerator for up to 2 days.

Tip

Dip your offset spatula in hot water when icing to give a smoother finish.

Get ahead

The spiced strawberries can be made in advance. The cake can be made a day in advance. Wrap well in plastic wrap once cool.

Turkish coffee creams

Coffee in Istanbul is not for the faint-hearted. It's deeply intense and bitter, with the remnants of coffee grounds lying at the bottom of your cup. The grounds can be used just like tea leaves to read your fortune. The syrup in this dessert gives the cream a serious coffee hit, just like the coffee I had in Istanbul. It's the ideal finale to a long meal.

For the coffee syrup

½ cup granulated sugar

6 tbsp water

2 tbsp brewed espresso

For the coffee cream

½ cup whole milk

10 tbsp brewed espresso

pinch of sea salt

3 egg yolks

6 tbsp granulated sugar

heaping 1 tbsp cornstarch

½ cup heavy cream

For the chocolate mendiants

3½ oz dark chocolate (70% cacao)

pinch of sea salt

2 tbsp pistachios, coarsely chopped

3 dried apricots, cut into thin strips

2 rose Turkish delights, cut into small pieces

To make the coffee syrup: Put the sugar and water in a small pan over low heat and bring to a simmer, swirling the pan. Simmer briskly for 5 minutes until thick and glossy. Add the espresso and pour into a small bowl. Let cool for about 20 minutes, or until room temperature, then chill in the refrigerator for 1 hour.

To make the coffee cream: Pour the milk and espresso into a pan over medium heat, add the salt, and bring it to scalding point. In the meantime, put the egg yolks and sugar into a bowl and whisk for 4 to 5 minutes, or until pale and fluffy, then fold in the cornstarch.

Slowly pour the hot coffee mixture over the egg mixture, whisking continuously. Transfer the mixture to a clean saucepan and continue to whisk over medium heat until the mixture releases a few bubbles and turns very thick and creamy. Remove from the heat, pour into a bowl, and put a piece of plastic wrap directly on the surface of the mixture to prevent a skin from forming. Let cool to room temperature, then place in the refrigerator to chill for 1 hour.

Beat the chilled coffee mixture to loosen it up. Whip the heavy cream to soft peaks and fold it into the coffee mixture. Spoon a heaping 1 tbsp into each glass, followed by 1 tsp of the coffee syrup. Alternate layers until the cream is used up (three to four layers per glass). Chill for about 2 hours, or until ready to serve.

To make the chocolate mendiants: Trace around the base of a serving glass six times on parchment paper. Place the paper on a baking sheet that will fit in your refrigerator.

Put the chocolate and salt in a heatproof bowl and melt over a pan of just-simmering water (don't let the bowl touch the water). Remove from the heat and set the chocolate aside for 15 minutes to thicken slightly. Spoon the chocolate onto the circles on the parchment paper (make them slightly smaller than the circles) and sprinkle each with some pistachios, apricots, and a piece of Turkish delight. Place in the refrigerator for at least 15 minutes to set.

To serve, top each cream with a mendiant lid.

Tips

Chocolate will separate when it is melted at too high a temperature. Make sure the water in the bottom of the double boiler doesn't boil when melting chocolate. If using the microwave, check and stir every few seconds.

The chocolate mix makes more than is required for the recipe, but these mendiants make wonderful edible gifts. They can be decorated with all sorts of dried fruit, nuts, chunks of soft toffee, and seeds.

If your mendiants are too big to fit into the glass, use a small cookie cutter to trim. Dip the cookie cutter in hot water first, dry, and use to cut. Don't press down too hard or the mendiant will crack. The heat of the cookie cutter will cut the chocolate.

Chocolate and zucchini fondant fancies

Makes 25 fondants	Preparation time: 30 minutes	Resting time: 1 hour	Baking time: 60 to 80 minutes

Don't be put off by the idea of zucchini in your cake. Like carrot, it makes for an extra-moist cake. The combination of hazelnut and chocolate reminds me of the famous store-bought spread; you could look at these fondants as a more wholesome and simplified variation.

4 eggs

1¼ cups granulated sugar

1¼ cups all-purpose flour

2½ cups ground blanched hazelnuts

4 tsp baking powder

pinch of sea salt

1⅓ lb zucchini, trimmed and very finely grated

14 oz dark chocolate (70% cacao), broken into pieces

¼ cup vegetable or sunflower oil, plus 1 tbsp

½ cup plus 1 tbsp confectioners' sugar

3½ oz white chocolate, broken into pieces

Preheat the oven to 325°F. Butter and flour a 9-in square pan.

Put the eggs and granulated sugar in a large bowl and whisk until thick and fluffy. In another bowl, mix together the flour, ground hazelnuts, baking powder, and salt. Add the flour mixture to the eggs and sugar and fold together quickly and lightly. Add the zucchini. Once they're incorporated evenly, pour the batter into the prepared pan.

Bake in the center of the oven for 60 to 80 minutes, or until a skewer comes out clean. Let cool for 5 minutes, then remove from the pan and transfer to a wire rack to cool completely. Refrigerate after it comes to room temperate, so it is firm upon cutting; this will help you get really straight edges on the cake.

Cut the cake into 1½-in squares. Set the squares on a wire rack set over parchment paper.

Meanwhile, melt the dark chocolate with the ¼ cup oil in a heatproof bowl set over a pan of just-simmering water (don't let the bowl touch the water). When melted, remove from the heat and stir in the confectioners' sugar. The icing should be runny enough to drip down the cake.

Place a piece of cake on a slotted spoon, fork, or angled spatula. Spoon over the chocolate icing evenly and leave to set on the wire rack for 30 minutes. If you find it easier, delicately ladle the chocolate icing over the top of the squares as they sit on the rack, letting the excess drip onto the parchment paper beneath (scooping up the icing to recycle for the other cakes).

Melt the white chocolate with the remaining 1 tbsp oil in a small heatproof bowl over a small pan of just-simmering water (don't let the bowl touch the water). Once the dark chocolate layer has set, drizzle the white chocolate decoration over the top and let set for 10 minutes. Serve within the day.

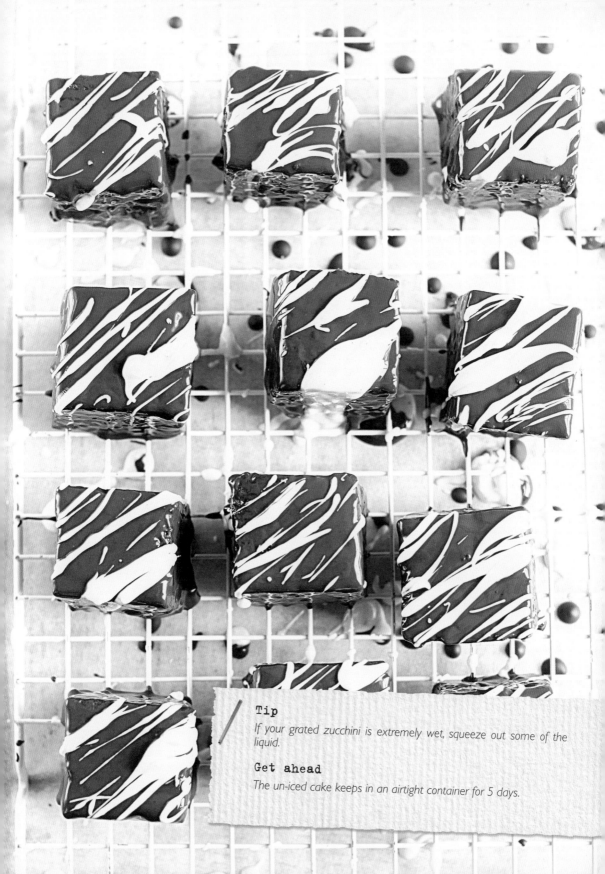

Tip
If your grated zucchini is extremely wet, squeeze out some of the liquid.

Get ahead
The un-iced cake keeps in an airtight container for 5 days.

Soft–serve ice cream with hazelnut caramel cone

Serves	Preparation time:	Cooking time:	Freezing time:
8	30 minutes	5 minutes	30 to 45 minutes

I love hearing the sound of the ice-cream truck. It reminds me of my childhood summers, when I would hound my mum to give me some money so I could buy a 99 Flake. I still love eating a 99 Flake (although I must admit the chocolate always tastes a little dusty). The ice cream, however, is light, super-smooth, and just dissolves in your mouth. You don't need a soft-serve machine in your kitchen to re-create the same experience, but a sugar thermometer, an electric mixer, and a piping bag with a tip are essential.

For the caramel sauce

¾ cup granulated sugar

½ cup plus 2 tbsp heavy cream

½ tsp sea salt

6 tbsp chopped hazelnuts, almonds, pecans, or walnuts, toasted

1 cup heavy cream

1 vanilla bean

2 tbsp water

6 tbsp granulated sugar

3 egg whites

8 ice cream waffle cones

2 tbsp chopped hazelnuts, almonds, pecans, or walnuts, toasted for serving

Get ahead

The caramel will keep for a couple of months in the refrigerator in a sterilized jar.

To make the caramel sauce: Sprinkle a thin layer of the sugar over the bottom of a heavy-bottomed pan and place over medium heat. Once the sugar starts to melt, add some more sugar. Repeat until all the sugar has melted, swirling the caramel around in the pan (do not stir). When it's almost a Coca-Cola color, turn down the heat and add the cream and salt (be careful, as the caramel may sputter). Cook for 1 to 2 minutes, until the temperature reaches 226°F on a digital thermometer. Watch it constantly. Take the caramel off the heat and let cool for a couple of minutes. Mix in the hazelnuts.

Put the heavy cream in a medium bowl. Halve the vanilla bean lengthwise and scrape out the seeds, then add them to the cream and whip until it forms soft peaks. Cover with plastic wrap and place in the refrigerator.

Pour the water and sugar into a small saucepan over high heat. Bring to a boil, swirling to melt the sugar. Meanwhile, put the egg whites in a large bowl and whisk with an electric hand mixer. Measure the temperature of the sugar syrup with a digital thermometer once it starts to boil, and when the sugar syrup reaches 258°F, slowly pour it into the egg whites while whisking at a high speed. Continue to whisk for about 5 minutes, or until you have a firm, thick meringue and the bowl is cool.

Fold the chilled whipped cream into the meringue. Spoon into a large piping bag fitted with a wide star tip. Make room in your freezer for eight tall glasses.

Place the waffle cones in the glasses and add a generous 1 tbsp of the caramel to each cone. Swirl each cone so that the caramel coats the inside, then pipe the cream into the cone in a spiral motion. Place back in the freezer for 30 to 45 minutes. Serve with a sprinkling of chopped hazelnuts.

Shake—and—make ice cream and toppings

Makes	Preparation time:	Freezing time:
1 qt	15 minutes	1 hour

You might think making ice cream at home requires an ice-cream machine or other gadgetry, but all you need are some kitchen trash bags, ¾ cup coarse sea salt, and 1¾ lb ice. Super–high tech! This is the way it was done in the past. I used an old ice-cream bucket when I worked in a restaurant in Sweden. It was a wooden bucket that you filled with ice and salt and it had a second container to put the ice-cream mix in. You then cranked a handle to turn the ice-cream ingredients around.

The salt brings the temperature of the ice down. Shaking the ice cream also helps the mix to cool down and makes it creamy. It's definitely a workout, but a fun thing to do with friends, when you can pass the effort around. Who would think that throwing some ingredients into a trash bag would make such a delicious result? Perhaps you'll have to try this for yourself to believe me!

2 cups heavy cream

2 cups whole milk

1¼ cups confectioners' sugar

1 vanilla bean, halved lengthwise and seeds scraped out

Place the cream, milk, confectioners' sugar, and vanilla bean seeds in a ziplock bag. Make sure it's well sealed before massaging it to combine the ingredients.

Put one trash-can liner inside a second one and place the ice and coarse salt inside. Shake a little before putting the ice-cream bag inside. Put your dishwashing gloves on. Shake the ice bag hard for at least 10 minutes, or until the mixture has set soft.

You can eat the ice cream immediately by squeezing it out of the bag into a container, but for a firmer consistency place in the freezer for 1 hour.

Tips
You can change the ratio of milk to cream for more or less creaminess. Add candied fruits, nuts, or chocolate chips for different flavorings.

Get ahead
Make the ice cream a few days ahead and store in the freezer until ready to serve.

Ice cream toppings

Makes enough for
8 sundaes

Preparation time:
40 minutes

Cooking time:
20 minutes

Chocolate and hazelnut sauce

3½ oz dark chocolate
(70% cacao)

¾ cup hazelnuts

2 tbsp unsalted butter

2 tbsp honey

pinch of sea salt

¾ cup heavy cream

Melt the chocolate in a heatproof bowl above a pan of just-simmering water (don't let the bowl touch the water). Grind the hazelnuts in a food processor as fine as possible.

Add the butter to the chocolate, along with the honey and salt. Heat the cream in a separate pan and pour over the chocolate. Stir together, add the hazelnuts, mix well, and serve.

Cherry compote

one 15-oz can pitted black
cherries in syrup

1 vanilla bean

½ tsp almond extract

Heat the cherries in their syrup in a pan. Split the vanilla bean, scrape out the seeds, and add them to the pan, along with the pod, then simmer for 10 minutes. Stir in the almond extract, remove the vanilla pod, and serve.

Caramel popcorn

½ tbsp salted butter

¼ cup popcorn kernels

For the salted butter caramel

⅓ cup granulated sugar

2 tbsp water

3 tbsp heavy cream

heaping 1 tbsp corn syrup

knob of unsalted butter

½ tsp sea salt

Melt the salted butter in a large pan with a lid over medium heat. Turn the heat to medium-high, add the popcorn kernels, and place the lid on the pan. When you hear the popcorn popping, start shaking the pan.

Shake the pan until it sounds like the kernels have stopped popping. Remove from the heat and set aside in a bowl.

To make the salted butter caramel: In a medium saucepan, combine half the sugar with the water. Place over high heat and let melt. Swirl the caramel around in the pan (do not stir). Once the caramel becomes a dark reddish brown, remove the pan from the heat and add the rest of the sugar, the cream, corn syrup, unsalted butter, and salt.

Put the saucepan back on the heat. Be careful not to stand over it as the caramel will steam and bubble a lot. Swirl the pan around before turning the heat to medium. Cook for 3 to 4 minutes, or until the caramel reaches 248°F on a digital thermometer and is rich, thick, and unctuous.

Stir the popcorn into the caramel, then spread the popcorn out on a lined baking sheet to cool. Store in an airtight container for up to 2 weeks. Break it up to serve.

Tropical knickerbocker glory

Serves	Preparation time:	Freezing time:	Cooking time:
4	40 minutes	6 hours	15 minutes

This recipe is a twist on one of my favorite Malaysian desserts, *cendol*. *Cendol* is a bright green sweet noodle, usually made with mung-bean flour and pandan leaf. The flavor and color come from the pandan leaf, which has an aromatic sweet almond and vanilla perfume. The noodles are then mixed with shaved ice and red beans and doused with coconut milk.

I've switched some of the ingredients (pandan leaf and mung-bean flour) for ones that are easy to buy in the supermarket (rice flour, cornstarch, and tropical fruit juice). There are no red beans in sight, but instead a colorful assortment of tropical fruits. No need for an ice machine to shave ice either; a quick-to-make coconut granita replaces that.

For the coconut granita

½ cup granulated sugar

6 tbsp water

one 13½-oz can coconut milk

For the tropical cendol

2½ tbsp rice flour

2½ tbsp cornstarch

1 cup tropical or exotic fruit juice

6 ripe passion fruits

½ small mango

½ cantaloupe

zest and juice of 1 lime

Tip

The granita can be made up to 3 weeks in advance. Just remove from the freezer for about 15 minutes before serving to soften if frozen solid.

To make the coconut granita: Dissolve the sugar in the water in a medium saucepan over low heat, swirling the pan gently. Bring to a simmer for 1 minute. Remove from the heat and stir in the coconut milk. Pour the mixture into a lidded plastic container. Place in the freezer for 6 hours, scraping the surface with the tines of a fork every hour or so after the first 2 hours (make sure you scrape the sides too; otherwise, it will freeze solid). Once the mixture is firm, cover or wrap tightly in plastic wrap.

To make the tropical cendol: Place the rice flour and cornstarch in a small saucepan. Whisk in the fruit juice, then cook over medium heat, whisking continuously, for 8 to 10 minutes, or until the mixture becomes very thick and glossy. Remove from the heat and leave for 2 minutes.

Prepare a large bowl of ice water. Transfer the cendol to a medium piping bag. Wearing dishwashing gloves (as the mixture in the bag is still very hot), pipe the cendol in long pieces straight into the ice water. Set aside for 15 minutes.

Meanwhile, remove the pulp from the passion fruits and put into a large bowl. Cut the mango and seed the cantaloupe, then chop the flesh into bite-size pieces. Toss the fruit with the lime zest and juice (saving a little zest for the garnish).

When ready to serve, scrape up the granita and place some at the bottom of four sundae glasses. Drain the water from the cendol and add some to each glass, then add a spoonful of fruit. Add another layer of granita, cendol, and fruit, then sprinkle with a little lime zest. Serve immediately.

Mini ice pops

Makes
16 pops

Preparation time:
5 minutes

Cooking time:
10 minutes

Freezing time:
2 hours

A DIY attitude is required for this recipe. I wanted to come up with an ice-pop mold that everyone could make out of things they would have at home: an ice-cube tray and cardboard (a cereal box works well). These little fruit pops are a refreshing way to finish a meal (similar to the ones that posh restaurants serve before dessert, to refresh the palate) or to have on a hot summer's day.

14 oz frozen mixed summer berries

½ cup plus 1 tbsp confectioners' sugar

1 tbsp chopped toasted hazelnuts

1 tbsp toasted caraway seeds

1 tbsp candy sprinkles

1 tbsp chocolate sprinkles

Cut a piece of cardboard to the size of the top of your ice-cube tray. Wrap the cardboard thoroughly in plastic wrap, place over the ice-cube tray, and use a utility knife or a pair of scissors to make 16 little slits in the cardboard over the center of the cubes on the tray.

Put the berries and confectioners' sugar in a medium saucepan over medium heat, cover, and cook for about 10 minutes. Transfer to a blender and blend until smooth, then pour through a sieve into a pitcher. Pour the mixture into the ice-cube tray. Place the cardboard lid on the ice-cube tray, secure with rubberbands, then insert lollipop sticks through the slits. Place in the freezer for 2 hours, or until frozen solid.

Remove from the freezer 10 minutes before serving and place in the refrigerator. Put the nuts, seeds, and sprinkles into separate bowls. When ready to serve, carefully remove the cardboard and dunk the fruit pops in your topping of choice.

Tip
Lightly oil the plastic wrap used to wrap the cardboard. This will help prevent the frozen ice pops from sticking.

Get ahead
The fruit pops can be made up to 3 weeks in advance.

Homemade Treats

Last, but certainly not least, I leave you with my final chapter. From cookies and Swedish-style buns to truffles and sweet chile sauce, even the most unstoppable of cooks (myself included) have been tempted to buy some of these rather than make them at home. But homemade is always so much better than store-bought, and while they might be more time-consuming to make, you'll definitely reap the rewards later.

From my time in France and beyond, the aperitif culture will always stick with me, and in this chapter you'll discover some impressive recipes for serving in that oft-neglected time before a meal. There's my home-cured duck breast (see page 220), from which you can simply slice off some slivers for an impromptu aperitif. Or my homemade grissini (see page 232), so unbelievably simple, you'll wonder why you never bothered making your own before.

Edible gifts come in many guises, and my Chocolate Bark (page 212) makes for a really speedy lunchbox treat for kids or even ever-so-lucky other halves. Then there are the cook's cheats to make everyday life a little bit more gourmet; take my Stock Cubes (page 248), or my Homemade Cottage Cheese (page 246) and put your own stamp on them when you use them.

This chapter is filled with a selection of recipes I have collected along the way, many of which have become my most trusted and most used. I hope they become yours too.

Chocolate bark

Serves
6

Preparation time:
5 minutes

Cooking time:
5 minutes

Cooling time:
1 hour

Making your own chocolate bark couldn't be simpler. Great for a snack, after-dinner chocolates, or the perfect edible gift.

7 oz dark chocolate (70% cacao), broken into pieces

2 tbsp mixed seeds (e.g., sunflower, pumpkin, and sesame)

2 tbsp dried cranberries

2 tbsp pistachios, coarsely chopped

Put the chocolate in a heatproof bowl and place over a pan of just-simmering water (don't let the bowl touch the water). Stir occasionally until melted. Line a rimmed baking sheet with parchment paper and pour the chocolate onto it, then spread with a spatula into a rectangle about 7 by 9 in and about ¾ in thick.

Immediately sprinkle the seeds, cranberries, and pistachios evenly over the top. Transfer to the refrigerator to set for at least 1 hour. Once set, break up the bark into jagged pieces to serve.

Tip
The toppings you can use for this are endless. I usually see what I have left over in my cupboard—from dried apricots, figs, or freeze-dried fruit (great for color) to hazelnuts, pecans, and sugar sprinkles.

Get ahead
Chocolate bark keeps in the refrigerator for up to 2 weeks.

Gorgonzola and ricotta sfogliatella

Makes
12 sfogliatella

Preparation time:
20 minutes

Baking time:
20 to 25 minutes

Making *sfogliatella* the traditional way is nearly as difficult as pronouncing the word. The traditional method calls for making a pastry and rolling it incredibly thinly. Then it is rolled up, chilled, formed into cone shapes, and filled with a semolina and ricotta cream that is studded with candied fruits ... basically, unless you have a large extended Italian family to help you with this, you'll be in the kitchen all day.

Not wanting to be defeated by a complicated technique, I set about finding a simple version that would still have the classic crispy layered pastry. Combining thinly rolled-out puff pastry and filo pastry seems to do the trick. I like to fill these with apple and a rich ricotta and Gorgonzola cream, which makes them perfect to kick off an evening of entertaining.

flour for rolling

7½ oz ready-rolled puff pastry

1 egg, beaten

2 sheets filo pastry (sheet size 12 by 16 in)

1 small apple

5 tbsp ricotta cheese

1¾ oz Gorgonzola cheese

Tip

If the puff pastry is very soft, put a sheet of parchment paper on top, roll it up, and place in the refrigerator for 10 minutes to firm up.

Preheat the oven to 350°F. Line a baking sheet with parchment paper. Dust your work surface with flour. Take the rectangle of puff pastry and place it with one short side facing you. Dust the top of the pastry with flour and roll out to the size of the sheet of filo pastry. The pastry should end up about ⅟₁₆ in thick. Sweep off the excess flour, then brush with some of the egg. Place a sheet of the filo over the top. Turn over and repeat with the other sheet of filo on the other side. Cut the pastry into 1-in strips using a pizza cutter.

Quarter and core the apple, then cut each quarter into two slices. Cut each slice in half, so you're left with pieces that have a wider end and a slimmer end. Mix the ricotta and Gorgonzola together in a small bowl.

Brush some of the egg all over the surface of a strip of pastry. Place a piece of apple at the end. Roll the strip up around the apple, making each fold slightly askew from the previous one. You will end up with a cone of pastry, with the apple at one end and a space at the other.

Press 1 tsp of the cheese mixture into the space, then seal both ends to encase the apple and cheese, using some egg to stick the pastry in place. Place on the prepared baking sheet and repeat with the remaining ingredients. Brush the outside of the pastries with egg.

Bake for 20 to 25 minutes, or until golden and crisp. Serve immediately.

Raw fig truffles

Makes	Preparation time:	Cooking time:	Chilling time:
12 truffles	20 minutes	5 minutes	1 hour

I love fresh figs; they're like candy for me. When I lived in Paris I would go to my local market and pick up a bag, and by the time I got home they would be gone. It's difficult to find perfectly ripe figs when they're not in season, so for the rest of the year I have to get my fig fix with the dried version. Dried figs are more intense and sweeter than the fresh ones, and pair beautifully with bitter dark chocolate.

½ cup dried figs

½ cup Medjool dates, pitted

5 tbsp pistachios

1½ tbsp unsalted butter, at room temperature

½ tsp sea salt

3½ oz dark chocolate (70% cacao)

¾ cup blanched almonds, toasted and finely chopped

Remove and discard the tough stalks from the tops of the figs. Chop the figs, then place in a food processor with the dates, pistachios, butter, and salt. Blend until they form a paste. Turn the paste out onto your work surface and roll into 12 small truffle-size balls, then place on a tray.

Put the chocolate in a heatproof bowl over a pan of just-simmering water (don't let the bowl touch the water). Let melt. Place the chopped almonds on a plate.

Dip the fig balls into the melted chocolate one at a time, using a couple of forks to coat well. Immediately transfer to the chopped almonds and roll to coat. Place on a plate or a small baking sheet lined with plastic wrap, then coat the remaining truffles. Put into the refrigerator to set for 1 hour before serving.

Tip
Experiment with other dried fruit or nuts to fill or coat your truffles.

Get ahead
These keep well in the refrigerator for up to 1 week in an airtight container. You can also freeze them before coating them with chocolate. They are good uncoated too.

Pine nut marzipan truffles

Makes	Preparation time:	Cooking time:
20 to 24 truffles	20 minutes	10 minutes

When you're planning the perfect meal, it's good to think about balance. Sometimes a traditional dessert, like a slice of cake or pudding, is just too heavy. Some homemade chocolate truffles and a small digestif, however, will stop your guests from feeling like they need to be forklifted home. Try my little pine nut marzipan truffles for a lighter finale, or make a double batch and offer them as excellent edible gifts.

2 heaping cups pine nuts, toasted

⅔ cup granulated sugar

⅔ cup confectioners' sugar

1 egg

½ cup ground almonds

generous pinch of sea salt

7 oz dark chocolate (70% cacao), chopped

Grind 1½ cups of the pine nuts in a blender until fine (but don't go so far that you end up with pine nut butter!).

Put a large heatproof bowl over a pan of just-simmering water (don't let the bowl touch the water). Place both sugars in the bowl, then whisk in the egg and continue whisking until the mixture turns pale and creamy. Remove from the heat and let cool a little.

Stir in the ground pine nuts, along with the almonds and salt, and continue stirring until you have a smooth marzipan and the mixture is thoroughly cool. Form the dough into little balls in the palm of your hand, about the size of truffles.

Bring the pan of water up to a simmer again. Place the chocolate in a clean heatproof bowl and melt it over the water.

Line a baking sheet with some plastic wrap. Dip the marzipan balls in the chocolate using a truffle fork, or simply dunk them in the chocolate and fish them out with a fork. Place on the prepared baking sheet and scatter with the remaining pine nuts. Let dry, then place in the refrigerator to set before serving.

Tip

If you find the flavor of the pine nuts too intense, you can blend a heaping 1 cup pine nuts and a heaping 1 cup almonds instead of 2 cups pine nuts to go in the marzipan balls.

You can also roll the coated truffles in finely chopped almonds.

Get ahead

These keep well in the refrigerator for a week or so in an airtight container. You can also freeze them.

Spiced duck ham

Makes
1 duck breast

Preparation time:
15 minutes

Curing time:
17 days

Making your own charcuterie couldn't be easier. The only thing you have to exercise is a little patience. As the saying goes, "All good things come to those who wait." (The duck has to hang for a little more than two weeks before it's ready.) But, at the end of this recipe, you'll be left with your own delicious cured duck breast. Serve with a fresh green salad or just on its own with some crusty bread and cornichons.

1¾ cup plus 2 tbsp coarse sea salt

2 cups granulated sugar

one 1-lb duck breast

2 tbsp freshly ground pepper

1 juniper berry, crushed

zest of 1 orange

Mix the salt and sugar together. Cut a large piece of plastic wrap and place half the salt-sugar mix in the middle. Place the duck breast on top. Cover the duck with the rest of the salt-sugar mix and wrap up tightly. Leave in the refrigerator for 72 hours.

Rinse the duck with cold water and pat dry with paper towels. Rub the spices and orange zest into the duck breast, then wrap it loosely in cheesecloth and hang it in the refrigerator. Leave for 14 days.

Unwrap and serve in very thin slices.

Tips

For a pepper coating, try a mixture of black, Szechuan, and white pepper. Make sure the meat is completely covered by the salt-sugar mix so that it dries out evenly.

Get ahead

The duck will continue to cure and dry in the refrigerator for up to 8 weeks.

Soft steamed buns

Makes 8 buns
(serves 4 as
a main course)

Preparation time:
40 minutes

Resting time:
1 hour 15 minutes

Cooking time:
30 to 40 minutes

Eating *char siu bao*, steamed Chinese buns filled with roast pork, was part of my childhood. The fluffy light dough encasing savory, sticky, and slightly sweet roast meat was one of my brother's and my favorites, growing up. The dumpling dough makes the perfect vehicle for using up leftovers. Serve some steamed broccoli on the side, and the buns are no longer simply a snack but a delicious meal in themselves.

For the filling

2 cups leftover roasted meat, such as pork

1 green onion, thinly sliced

½ carrot, cut into ¼-in cubes

1 tbsp tomato purée

1 tbsp light soy sauce

½ tsp freshly ground pepper

For the bun dough

1⅓ cups all-purpose flour

1 tbsp powdered milk

1½ tbsp granulated sugar

scant 1 tsp fast-acting yeast

1 tsp baking powder

pinch of sea salt

6 tbsp warm water

2 tbsp vegetable oil

2 cups good-quality beef stock or other stock, depending on meat used

Sweet Chile Sauce (page 251) for serving

To make the filling: Trim the fat from the leftover roasted meat, then cut the meat into ¼-in cubes. Put the meat in a small bowl; add the green onion, carrot, tomato purée, soy sauce, and pepper; and mix well.

To make the bun dough: Combine the flour, powdered milk, sugar, yeast, baking powder, and salt in a large bowl. Mix together, then make a well in the center and add the warm water. Use a spoon to bring together, then turn out and knead for 2 to 3 minutes, or until you have a smooth dough. Place in an oiled bowl and cover with a kitchen towel or plastic wrap. Let rise for 45 minutes, or until nearly doubled in size.

Dust your work surface and your hands with flour. Divide the dough into two. Roll the first piece into a fat sausage and cut it into four equal parts. Roll each part into a ball, then flatten into a circle. Put a heaping 1 tbsp of filling into the middle of each one. Stretch the dough over the filling and squeeze the top together to seal. Dip the tops of the dumplings in flour (to prevent them from sticking) and place seam-side down on a baking sheet. Repeat with the rest of the dough. Let rise for 30 minutes.

Heat the oil in a large nonstick pan with a vented lid over medium heat. Place the buns, seam-side down, in the pan and fry for a couple of minutes, or until they have developed a golden crust on the bottom. Add the stock, bring to a boil, and cover with the lid. Cook for 30 to 40 minutes, or until you hear a sizzling noise. This means the stock has evaporated. Cook for another minute to crisp up the base of the buns, then serve immediately with spoonfuls of chile sauce.

Tip

For a vegetarian version, replace the meat with finely chopped button mushrooms.

Lemon, dill and fish roe bullar

Makes	Preparation time:	Rising time:	Cooking time:
22 to 24 buns	20 minutes	1½ hours	20 minutes

The Swedes love their buns. You can't go into a bakery, café, or petrol station without finding a *kanelbulle* or *kardemummabulle* (cinnamon bun or cardamom bun). *Bulle*, quite simply, means "bun" or "ball" (Swedish meatballs are called *köttbullar*, for instance). These savory versions make a great snack on the go, and use some of the perennial flavors found in Swedish cuisine: dill, lemon, and fish roe.

I cup plus 2 tbsp lukewarm whole milk

6 tbsp granulated sugar

½ tsp sea salt

6 tbsp unsalted butter, melted

2 eggs

2 tsp fast-acting yeast

4 cups all-purpose bread flour, plus more as necessary

14 oz cream cheese

4 tbsp finely chopped fresh dill

zest of 1 unwaxed lemon

6 tbsp lumpfish caviar

Mix the milk, sugar, salt, butter, 1 egg, and yeast together in the bowl of a stand mixer fitted with the dough hook. When combined, add the flour in two batches. Knead for 10 minutes until the dough comes together, adding a little more flour if necessary.

When the dough is nice and stretchy, form it into a ball with your hands. Cover with a clean damp kitchen towel or cloth and set aside in a warmish place for about 1 hour, or until it doubles in size.

Dust your work surface lightly with flour. Divide the dough into two balls (I find this easier to roll out in two batches; alternatively, you can just save the other half for another day).

Roll the dough into a rectangle about 16 by 14 in and ¼ in thick. Spread half the cream cheese in an even layer on top, then sprinkle on half the dill, half the lemon zest, and dot with half the fish roe.

Fold the filled dough into thirds lengthwise, first lifting a third of the dough toward the middle, then folding the top third down so it aligns with the bottom edge of the dough. Cut the dough into strips about 1¼ in wide using a pizza cutter or knife, then cut each strip down the middle until ¾ in from the top, as if you're making a pair of pants. Twist each strip, then twist each pair of strips together and into a bun shape, tucking the ends underneath. Place on a baking sheet lined with parchment paper. Repeat with the remaining dough. Beat the second egg, brush over the buns, and set them aside to rise for about 30 minutes, or until puffed. Brush with egg a second time.

Preheat the oven to 400°F.

Bake for 15 to 20 minutes, until golden. Place on a wire rack and let cool. These are best eaten slightly warm and fresh on the same day they're baked.

Tip

For the traditional kanelbullar (cinnamon buns), replace the topping ingredients with 1¼ cups butter, ¾ cup light brown sugar, and 2 tbsp ground cinnamon. Beat the ingredients together before spreading on top of dough, then proceed as directed.

Savory gems

Makes 50 crackers	Preparation time: 45 minutes	Cooking time: 10 to 12 minutes

Iced gems—little round cookies topped with candy-colored icing—were very hard to resist when I was a kid. When I tasted them recently, however, I realized how easily satisfied I was with food as a child. Although store-bought ones can be a little disappointing, homemade savory ones are the perfect way to kick off a party. These bite-size buttery crackers topped with colorful (all natural!) toppings are a treat for both old and young.

For the cracker bases

⅔ cup all-purpose flour

½ cup whole-wheat flour

½ tsp sea salt

1 tbsp granulated sugar

1 tsp paprika

6 tbsp cold butter, cubed

2 tsp vodka

For the deviled egg cream

3 eggs

2 tbsp Mayonnaise (page 249)

1 tsp English mustard

sea salt and freshly ground pepper

For the avocado cream

1 ripe avocado

1 tsp lime juice or lemon juice

pinch of salt

For the harissa cream cheese

1 tsp harissa paste

3½ oz cream cheese or mascarpone cheese

To make the cracker bases: Preheat the oven to 325°F. Line a baking sheet with parchment paper. Mix together both flours, the salt, sugar, and paprika in a large bowl, then rub in the butter with your fingers until you have a sandy texture. Add the vodka and bring the mixture together into a ball. Roll out with a rolling pin to ¼ in thick between two sheets of parchment paper.

With a cookie cutter, stamp out 50 crackers, re-rolling the dough as necessary, and put on the prepared baking sheet. Bake for 10 to 12 minutes, or until golden. Remove from the oven and transfer to a wire rack to cool.

To make the deviled egg cream: Place the eggs in a pan of boiling water and boil for 10 minutes. Remove with a slotted spoon and run under cold water to cool. Peel the eggs and separate the yolks from the whites (discarding the whites). Mix the yolks with the mayonnaise and mustard and season with salt and pepper. Using a food processor, blend to a purée and set aside.

To make the avocado cream: Scoop the flesh out of the avocado into a small bowl, add the lime juice and salt, and mix and blend to a purée.

To make the harissa cream cheese: Mix the harissa into the cream cheese and blend into a purée.

Place the deviled egg cream in a piping bag fitted with a star tip and pipe little blobs onto one-third of the cooled crackers. Clean the tip, then repeat with the other toppings and crackers. Transfer to a platter and serve.

Tips

If the pastry becomes too soft when handling, place in the freezer for 5 minutes and run your hands under cold water.

Adding vodka to the pastry will make for a flakier pastry than using ice-cold water. The alcohol evaporates when baked.

Mini focaccia buns

Makes 10 buns	Preparation time: 20 minutes	Rising time: 1 hour	Baking time: 20 minutes
🍴🍽️			

The Italians, like the French, are strong supporters of tradition, particularly when it comes to gastronomy and timeless recipes. So apologies in advance for these delightful little focaccia buns, which I doubt you will have previously encountered in a trattoria. Being small, these buns take a lot less time to proof and bake, meaning there will be fresh bread on the table quicker than you can say *mamma mia*. They are also great for using up all those little bits lurking in the back of the refrigerator.

2 cups white bread flour

1 tsp fast-acting yeast

sea salt

⅔ cup lukewarm water

olive oil for drizzling

various garnishes, such as cubed cheese (e.g., taleggio, goat's cheese, Gorgonzola), fresh rosemary, olives, thinly sliced garlic, marinated tomatoes or artichokes, jalapeños, cubes of cooked potato or butternut squash

In a large bowl, mix together the flour, yeast, and 1 tsp salt. Make a well in the middle and pour in the water. Mix until you have a rough dough. Turn out and knead for about 10 minutes, or until soft and smooth.

Place in an oiled bowl and cover with a clean damp kitchen towel. Leave to rise in a warm place for 30 minutes, or until doubled in size.

Punch down the dough. Roll into a sausage on a lightly floured surface and cut into ten pieces, then roll each piece into a ball. Poke your thumb in the middle to make a hole, drizzle with 1 tsp olive oil, and stick in the garnish of your choice. Make sure to press the garnish down very firmly (the buns will puff up and push out the garnish otherwise). Place them on a baking sheet lined with parchment paper. Let rise for 30 minutes, or until doubled in size.

Preheat the oven to 400°F.

Firmly push the garnish into the bun once more and drizzle with a little more olive oil. Sprinkle with salt.

Bake for 20 minutes, or until golden. Tap the base of a roll to check if it is done; it should sound hollow. Let cool on a rack before serving.

Get ahead

The dough can be left overnight in the refrigerator for the first rise.

The buns keep for up to 2 days; reheat in a 200°F oven to freshen them up.

The baked buns also freeze well. Defrost and reheat in a 300°F oven.

Grissini

Makes 16 to 25 grissini	Preparation time: 15 minutes	Resting time: 1 to 2 hours	Baking time: 12 to 15 minutes

Italy's cuisine, like that of France, is considered one of the world's greatest, and although I haven't spent nearly as much time in Italy as I have in France, I'm very fond of the food. I do have one pet peeve, however, which I discovered while eating out on many of my trips there: those mass-produced, plastic-packaged grissini sticks that are served in bread baskets at restaurants. These grissini are dry, flavorless, and, for me, like eating compressed sawdust. Anyway, enough ranting! I decided to put together a mini guide on how to make the most fantastic array of grissini, fit for a king's or queen's bread basket.

2 cups unbleached bread flour

½ tsp fast-acting yeast

¾ tsp sea salt

½ tsp granulated sugar

⅔ cup warm water

Mix the flour, yeast, salt, and sugar in a large bowl, make a well in the center, and pour in the warm water. Stir the ingredients together, then use your hand to knead the mixture for about 5 minutes. The dough will be quite wet, but don't be tempted to add flour; the more you knead it, the less wet it will become. When the dough comes together into a small ball (but is still sticky), place it in a lightly oiled bowl. Cover with plastic wrap and leave in a warm place for 1 hour, until it doubles in size.

Preheat the oven to 400°F. Line a baking sheet with parchment paper.

Dust the work surface with flour and roll out the dough to a 10 by 12 in rectangle, about ½ in thick. Cut with a pizza cutter into ½-in-wide strips. Place the strips on the prepared baking sheet, leaving ¾ in between them.

Bake in the oven on the middle rack for 12 to 15 minutes, or until golden and crisp. Transfer to a wire rack and let cool slightly before eating. Wait until completely cool before storing in an airtight container for up to 3 days.

Apple and fig

½ apple, cut into cubes

3 dried figs, hard knobbly bit removed, thinly sliced

1 recipe basic dough (above)

Add the apple cubes and dried figs to the dough after mixing in the water and before kneading. Proceed as directed.

Rye, caraway, and Cheddar

½ cup plus 2 tbsp rye flour

1½ cups unbleached bread flour

½ tsp fast-acting yeast

¾ tsp sea salt

½ tsp granulated sugar

⅔ cup warm water

2¾ oz aged Cheddar, cut into small cubes

1½ tsp caraway seeds

Mix both flours, the yeast, salt, and sugar in a large bowl, then add the water, stir, and knead as in the basic grissini recipe. Add the Cheddar and 1 tsp of the caraway seeds toward the end of the kneading time so that they are evenly incorporated. Let the dough rest, then roll it out to a 10-in square and cut into 16 strips roughly ¾ wide. Scatter with the remaining caraway seeds, pressing them in lightly. Spread out on a prepared baking sheet, then bake cool as directed.

Raspberry and dark chocolate

3½ oz raspberries

¼ cup warm water

2 cups unbleached bread flour

½ tsp fast-acting yeast

½ tsp sea salt

1 tbsp granulated sugar

7 oz dark chocolate (70% cacao)

Place the raspberries in the warm water and crush lightly with a fork. Mix the flour, yeast, salt, and sugar in a large bowl. Add the raspberries and their liquid, then stir and knead. Let the dough rest, then roll out and bake as directed for the grissini. Once baked, let cool slightly.

Cut the chocolate into small pieces and place in a heatproof bowl above a pan of just-simmering water (don't let the bowl touch the water). Use a spoon to drizzle the melted chocolate over half of each of the breadsticks. Let set in the refrigerator for 15 minutes before serving.

Pistachio, sesame, white chocolate, and wasabi

2½ cups unbleached bread flour

scant ¼ cup pistachios

½ tsp fast-acting yeast

¾ tsp sea salt

½ tsp granulated sugar

⅔ cup warm water

1 tbsp black sesame seeds

3½ oz white chocolate

2 tsp wasabi powder

Mix the flour, pistachios, yeast, salt, and sugar in a large bowl. Add the water, then stir and knead. Let the dough rest, then roll it out into a 10-in square and cut into 16 strips roughly ¾ in wide. Scatter with the sesame seeds. Spread out on a prepared baking sheet, and bake and cool as directed. Once baked, let cool slightly.

Cut the chocolate into small pieces and place in a heatproof bowl above a pan of just-simmering water (don't let the bowl touch the water). Add the wasabi and stir. Use a spoon to drizzle the melted chocolate haphazardly over the top of the breadsticks. Leave to set in the refrigerator for 15 minutes before serving.

continued

Raspberry and dark chocolate

Apple and fig

Grissini

Pistachio, sesame, white chocolate, and wasabi

Pizza grissini

1 tsp tomato purée

½ cup plus 2 tbsp warm water

2 cups unbleached bread flour

½ tsp fast-acting yeast

¾ tsp sea salt

½ tsp granulated sugar

1¾ oz sun-dried tomatoes, finely chopped

1 tbsp dried oregano

Mix the tomato purée with the water in a small bowl. Mix the flour, yeast, salt, and sugar in a separate large bowl. Add the sun-dried tomatoes, oregano, and tomato purée, then stir and knead. Let the dough rest, then roll out and bake as directed on page 232.

No-knead herby gluten-free grissini

3¼ cups gluten-free plain white flour blend

1 tsp fast-acting yeast

1½ tsp sea salt

2 tsp granulated sugar

2 tsp nigella seeds

2 tsp dried mint

2 tsp dried thyme

1¼ cups warm water

1 egg, beaten

Mix the dry ingredients together in a large bowl and add the water, mixing together until well incorporated. Roll into a ball and leave to rest for 2 hours in a lightly oiled bowl covered with plastic wrap.

Preheat the oven to 400°F. Line a baking sheet with parchment paper.

Remove the dough from the bowl and divide into twenty pieces. Roll each piece into a ball, then into the shape of a breadstick. Place on the prepared baking sheet and brush with the egg, then bake as directed on page 232.

Tips

Grissini are great as both a sweet and a savory finger food. Here are some ideas to tart up your basic breadsticks for a party.

• *Stick the following on the end of them: raspberries; hard-boiled quail eggs dipped in sesame seeds; mozzarella cheese bocconcini*

• *Wrap them in melon ribbons and Parma ham*

• *Spread cream cheese along one end, then wrap peeled apple ribbons around the tip*

Rye and molasses quick bread with whipped homemade butter

Preparation time:
15 minutes

Cooking time:
30 minutes

This is the perfect loaf for those with limited patience who love fresh bread. Unlike a traditional loaf, this bread relies on baking soda rather than yeast for its leavening, and needs as little mixing as possible to make a soft and tender crumb. With a slightly sweet and bitter note from the molasses, it goes down like a treat when warm and buttered. Homemade butter might seem like taking it too far but there's nothing to it apart from overwhipping the cream (plus, the buttermilk comes in handy for the bread).

For the whipped butter

2 cups heavy cream

2 pinches of sea salt

3 tbsp finely chopped chives

1 cup all-purpose flour

1 cup rye or whole-wheat flour

1 tsp baking soda

1 tbsp firmly packed light brown sugar

1 tsp ground sea salt flakes

2 to 5 tbsp plain yogurt

3½ tbsp molasses

1 tbsp rolled oats

To make the whipped butter: In the bowl of a stand mixer fitted with the whisk attachment, whisk the cream on high speed until it separates to butter solids and buttermilk—this takes about 5 minutes. Drain off the buttermilk and set aside. Continue to whip the remaining butter until soft and fluffy, adding the salt and chopped chives when the mixture begins to form into butter.

Preheat the oven to 350°F. Butter and flour a 9-in loaf pan.

Mix together both flours, the baking soda, brown sugar, and salt in a large bowl. Make a well in the center. Measure out the buttermilk and add enough yogurt to total ¾ cup plus 2 tbsp. Pour the buttermilk and yogurt into the center of the dry ingredients, mix together, and add the molasses. Mix until everything is incorporated. Try not to overwork it. Put the mixture into the prepared pan and spread it out so that it is level. Sprinkle with the oats.

Bake for 30 minutes, or until a skewer comes out clean from the center. Let cool for 5 minutes before removing from the pan. Cover with a damp kitchen towel while cooling. Serve with the butter on the side.

Tips

Best eaten while warm or the following day, toasted.

If you want to avoid making the butter, replace the buttermilk and yogurt in the bread recipe with a combination of 7 tbsp whole milk and 7 tbsp plain yogurt.

Dark chocolate and cherry cookies

Makes	Preparation time:	Freezing time:	Baking time:
16 cookies	10 minutes	30 to 45 minutes	12 to 14 minutes

I woke up one morning with an overwhelming craving for a deep dark chocolate cookie studded with cherries. Most important, it had to have the right texture—crisp on the edges and chewy in the middle. A few factors are involved in making the perfect chewy cookie: baking for the right amount of time at the right temperature and using dark brown sugar, which makes for a moister cookie.

½ cup salted butter

6 tbsp dark brown sugar

6 tbsp light brown sugar

½ tsp sea salt

⅔ cup plus 2 tbsp all-purpose flour

2½ tbsp cocoa powder

½ tsp baking powder

1 egg

½ tsp almond extract

3½ oz dark chocolate (70% cacao), roughly chopped into small pieces

3½ oz dried cherries, chopped in half

Melt the butter, both sugars, and salt in a medium saucepan, then let cool slightly.

Sift the flour, cocoa powder, and baking powder into a bowl and mix together. Make a well in the center, add the egg and almond extract, and begin to mix. Pour in the slightly cooled butter-sugar mixture. Mix together until there are no lumps.

Lay out a large piece of plastic wrap on a small baking sheet on your work surface. Pour the batter onto the plastic wrap and spread it into a neat square, about ¾ in thick. Use the excess wrap to cover the dough and place in the freezer on the baking sheet for 30 to 45 minutes (or in the refrigerator for 1 to 2 hours), until firm enough to cut into 16 squares.

Preheat the oven to 325°F. Line two large baking sheets with parchment paper.

Place the dough squares on the prepared baking sheets, leaving a 1-in gap between each cookie (they will spread out a fair bit as they bake). Press the chocolate and cherries lightly into the squares. Bake for 12 to 14 minutes, or until slightly crisp on the outside but still soft in the middle (they will harden as they cool). Leave on the baking sheet for 10 minutes, then use a spatula to transfer to a wire rack to cool completely. These are best eaten on the day you bake them.

Tip
For a plain cookie, replace the cocoa powder with all-purpose flour. The cherries and chocolate can be replaced with other flavorings, such as white chocolate and dried cranberries, or dark chocolate and walnuts.

Get ahead
The cookies freeze well, either baked or as a dough. Add an extra 5 minutes to the baking time if frozen.

THESE WILD GARLIC FLOWERS
WOULD BE DELICIOUS
IN AN OMELETTE

STRAWBERRIES -
PERFECT FOR CAKE RECIPE

LOVE THE NAME OF
THESE CUCUMBERS

MY KIND OF HEAVEN -
CHEESE!

NOTHING BEATS GETTING A
BEAUTIFUL BUNCH OF FLOWERS

OYSTERS WITH A
BLOODY MARY DRESSING

HUGE SEAFOOD PLATTER

A SMALL HANDFUL
OF LINGONBERRIES -
ENOUGH FOR ME ☺

AMAZING WHAT YOU CAN
GROW IN A WINDOW BOX

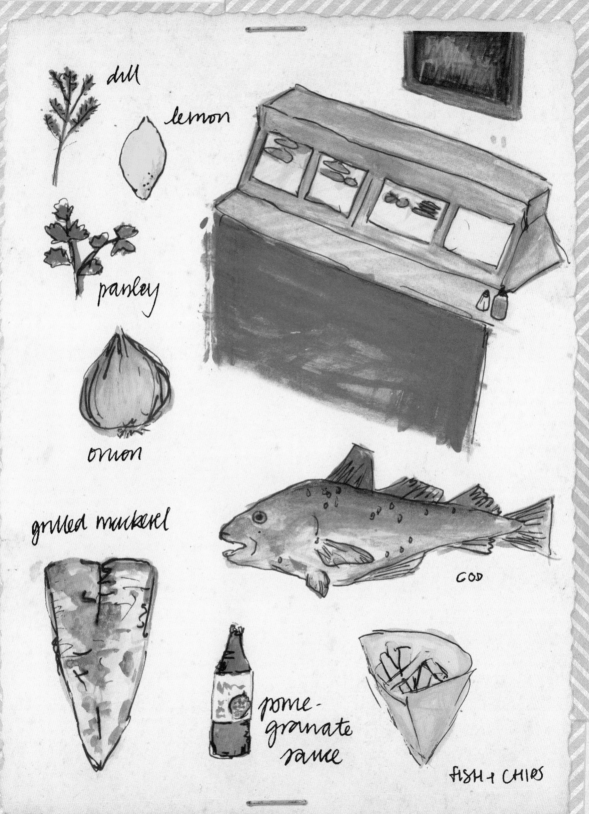

dill

lemon

parsley

onion

grilled mackerel

COD

pome-
granate
sauce

FISH + CHIPS

Potato churros with red pepper sauce

Makes 20 churros, plus 1¼ cups sauce

Preparation time: 30 minutes

Cooling time: 20 minutes

Cooking time: 40 minutes

When I was in Barcelona I visited a classic *churrería*, which felt like the local spot to gather—a bit like the local café where you would grab a cup of tea and catch up with the latest gossip. It was cheap and cheerful, and they made sinfully good churros, served with rich hot chocolate so thick that you could stand them up in it. Although they are traditionally a breakfast food, if you switch an ingredient or two they make a great savory dish.

5 tbsp butter

⅔ cup plus 2 tbsp potato flour

⅔ cup plus 2 tbsp all-purpose flour

1 tsp granulated sugar

½ tsp sea salt

¼ tsp baking powder

2 eggs

For the red pepper sauce

4 red bell peppers

1 clove of garlic, peeled

1 tbsp extra-virgin olive oil

6 cherry tomatoes

sea salt and freshly ground pepper

4½ cups sunflower or vegetable oil

½ tsp sweet smoked paprika

Melt the butter in a medium saucepan and, when it starts to bubble, gently beat in both flours, the sugar, salt, and baking powder. Mix with a wooden spoon until it comes together, then crack in the eggs one by one and mix again. Place the batter in a piping bag fitted with a star-shaped tip, and chill in the refrigerator.

To make the red pepper sauce: Preheat the broiler. Cut the bell peppers in half and remove the seeds. Place skin-side up on an oiled baking sheet and broil for 15 to 20 minutes, or until blackened and tender. Place in a plastic bag and set aside to steam for about 20 minutes.

When the peppers are cool enough to handle, remove and discard the skins and place the flesh in a blender with the garlic, olive oil, and tomatoes. Blend until very smooth. Season with salt and pepper.

Heat the sunflower oil in a large heavy pot over high heat until it is 350°F. Test the temperature with a tiny amount of the batter. If it fizzes when it hits the oil, you are ready to start frying.

Pipe the batter directly into the hot oil. Use a pair of scissors to snip each churro at the piping tip when it's about 4 in long. Pipe out 10 churros. Fry the churros for 5 to 6 minutes, or until lightly pale golden. They will need to be turned carefully a few times with a long-handled slotted spoon.

Drain the churros on paper towels. Sprinkle with a little smoked paprika while still hot. Repeat until all the batter has been cooked. Serve with the red pepper sauce on the side.

Get ahead

The sauce can be made in advance, but the churros are best eaten hot from the oil.

Homemade cottage cheese

Makes
1⅓ cups

Preparation time:
15 minutes

Resting time:
1 hour

Making your own cottage cheese might seem a little unnecessary but the homemade stuff is nothing like the store-bought variety. It makes the perfect base for my English Garden Salad (page 42).

9 cups whole milk

sea salt and freshly ground pepper

juice of 4 lemons

In a large pan, heat the milk with a sprinkle of salt and a few grinds of pepper. Just before it comes to a boil, remove it from the heat. Stir in the lemon juice, then cover and set aside for 30 minutes. The milk will curdle and separate into whey and curd.

Pour the mixture through a sieve lined with cheesecloth. Hang the cheesecloth over the sink for the curd to drain for about 30 minutes. When drained, twist the cheesecloth around the top of the cheese and squeeze it dry. Store for a couple of days in the refrigerator in an airtight container.

3 ways with cottage cheese

Chunky tomato cottage cheese

8 cherry tomatoes

1⅓ cups Homemade Cottage Cheese (facing page)

sea salt and freshly ground pepper

tortilla chips for serving

Finely chop the tomatoes. Season the cottage cheese with salt and pepper and place in a serving bowl. Scatter the tomatoes on top and serve with tortilla chips.

Herby cottage cheese

1⅓ cups Homemade Cottage Cheese (facing page)

½ cup crème fraîche or Greek yogurt

1 small bunch chives or other herbs, finely chopped

pinch of salt (optional)

½ tsp freshly ground pepper (optional)

Put the cottage cheese in a large bowl and mix with the crème fraîche and herbs. Season with the salt and pepper, if desired.

Sweet and seedy cottage cheese

1⅓ cups Homemade Cottage Cheese (facing page)

6 tbsp Greek yogurt

4 tbsp mixed seeds (pumpkin, hemp, linseed, sesame), toasted

4 tbsp honey

Put the cottage cheese in a large bowl and mix with the Greek yogurt. In a separate bowl, mix the toasted seeds with the honey. Divide the cheese mixture among four bowls and serve each with a dollop of the honey and seeds in the middle.

Tips

Cottage cheese can be flavored with many different herbs and spices, such as chopped basil, parsley, cilantro, or sweet and smoky paprika.

You can serve the sweet version with fresh fruit and granola.

Stock cubes

Makes	Cooking time:	Preparation time:
14 cubes	45 minutes	2 minutes

Having good stock on hand means having a constant source of flavor to play with. But in a small kitchen it can be tricky to store fresh stock all the time. Reducing stock down until it's intensely concentrated, then freezing it in ice-cube trays is a great way of making it available for any occasion, without taking up too much precious space.

4½ cups fresh ham stock
(see page 93)

Place the stock in a large wide pan and simmer for about 45 minutes, or until reduced to about ¾ cup. Pour into an empty ice-cube tray and let cool before placing in the freezer until solid. Store in an airtight container in the freezer for up to 2 months.

Tip
You can use this stock whenever you like; it's perfect for my Speedy One-Pot Noodle (page 102).

Mayonnaise

Makes about 1 cup

¶ O¶

3 egg yolks, at room
temperature

¾ to 1 cup sunflower or
vegetable oil (or 6 to 8 tbsp
olive oil, if you prefer a
peppery taste)

2 tsp white wine vinegar or
lemon juice

sea salt

Place the egg yolks in a large glass or stainless-steel bowl set on a
damp tea towel (to stop the bowl from slipping). Whisk the yolks
a little, then add the oil drop by drop, whisking continuously, until
the eggs begin to thicken and become pale. Continue drizzling the
oil into the mixture until you have achieved the consistency you
like. Add a few drops of vinegar and season with salt. Store in an
airtight container in the refrigerator for up to 1 week.

Tip

To flavor your mayonnaise, stir in 1 to 2 tbsp of harissa (to taste)
for a spicy kick, or 1 tbsp of lemon, orange, or grapefruit zest for
a zingy twist.

Tartar sauce

Makes about 1¼ cups

¶ O¶

1 tbsp each chopped capers,
chopped cornichons, chopped
parsley, chopped tarragon, and
chopped chervil

1 recipe Mayonnaise (above)

Stir the capers, cornichons and herbs into the mayonnaise. Store
in an airtight container in the refrigerator for up to 2 days.

Sweet chile sauce

Makes about 1²/₃ cups	Preparation time: 5 minutes	Cooking time: 15 minutes	Cooling time: 30 minutes

I have quite a collection of chile sauces in my refrigerator, from the super-fiery stuff to this one, which you can pretty much put on anything if you fancy a sweet and spicy kick.

¾ cup water

1 cup granulated sugar

¾ cup white wine vinegar

one 1-in piece ginger, peeled and finely chopped

3 to 4 small red chiles, very finely chopped, with seeds

1 tbsp cornstarch

Place the water in a small saucepan over high heat with the sugar, vinegar, ginger, and chiles. Bring to a boil, then continue to boil for 10 minutes, stirring occasionally.

Whisk 1½ tbsp of the liquid into the cornstarch in a small bowl, then add back to the saucepan. Turn the heat to low and cook, stirring continuously with a wooden spoon, for about 5 minutes, until it thickens to a just-pourable consistency. Decant into sterilized jars and leave for about 30 minutes to cool completely. Store in the refrigerator for up to 1 month.

Tip

Depending on the heat of the chiles and your personal preference, you can adjust the number used and remove the seeds if desired.

Get ahead

To sterilize glass jars, wash thoroughly and drain upside down. Place on a baking sheet in a 350°F oven for 10 minutes. Sterilize the lids by placing in boiling water for 10 minutes, then remove carefully and let dry on clean kitchen towels.

Miso toffee cherry tomatoes

Makes
20 tomatoes

Preparation time:
10 minutes

Cooking time:
15 minutes

I love to play around with sweet and savory flavors. I first tasted a version of this recipe in a French-Japanese restaurant in Nice. I loved the way this little appetizer looked. Very chic! The French name *tomates d'amour* (love tomatoes) had me too. The miso adds a little saltiness to the caramel and works so well (just think salted butter caramel).

20 cherry tomatoes

2 tbsp furikake* or a mix of white and black sesame seeds

2 tbsp sweet white miso paste

6 tbsp hot water

1½ cups granulated sugar

A mix of black and white sesame seeds, seaweeds, and dried shiso leaves. Found in Asian supermarkets or online.

Line a baking sheet with parchment paper. Wash and dry the cherry tomatoes, then stick them on the ends of individual bamboo skewers. Put the furikake in a ramekin or small bowl.

Dilute the miso paste in the hot water and place in a medium saucepan over medium heat. Add the sugar and let dissolve—do not stir, but swirl the pan around if needed. When the sugar has fully dissolved, simmer until it reaches 300°F and becomes a light rusty brown. Remove from the heat.

Quickly submerge the skewered tomatoes completely in the caramel. Let the excess drip off before immediately dipping into the furikake and placing on the prepared baking sheet. Let set for 5 minutes before serving.

Tips

Use a light-colored saucepan as it's easier to see the color of the caramel changing.

Don't wait too long before dipping the candied tomatoes into the furikake; otherwise, the furikake won't stick.

When cleaning your saucepan, put plenty of water in it and return to the heat; the caramel will dissolve and you can pour it away.

Get ahead

Don't make these more than a couple of hours in advance, as the toffee will soften with the humidity in the air.

large cocotte

large frying pan

speed
peeler

small pot

stainless-steel
mixing bowls

heatproof
spatula

digital
scale

knives

Equipment

I've always believed that you don't need the latest gadgets and gizmos to make a delicious meal, and have often cooked in places where not everything is at hand. I've built up my kitchen equipment over the years, but if I had to do it all over again on a small budget these are the things I would initially invest in:

Large Dutch oven or cocotte
Perfect for slow cooking dishes. Also great because you can transfer it from stove top to oven. Not the cheapest item to buy, but a good-quality one will last you a lifetime. I've found a few that are in good condition at thrift shops and flea markets.

Large frying pan
Invest in one with a heavy bottom (it conducts the heat better) and a good-quality handle (usually the first thing to break).

Small saucepan
For the smaller jobs where you don't need a large stockpot.

Speed peeler
One of my favorite tools, not because I love peeling potatoes but because you can use it to make ribbons out of cucumbers, zucchini, carrots, and many other things to jazz up your salads.

Small and large stainless-steel or glass mixing bowls
Plastic bowls are harder to get super-clean. They're more likely to have traces of grease from being used beforehand, which is the last thing you want when you're making a meringue. A spotless bowl is essential for making meringues, and stainless-steel or glass mixing bowls are perfect for this. They also come in handy for melting chocolate over a pan of simmering water.

A chef's knife, a serrated bread knife, and a small paring knife, plus a knife sharpener
If there's one thing you should spend money on, it's knives. Well looked after and kept sharp, they should last you at least a decade, if not a lifetime. Make sure to store your knives in a knife block or on a magnetic knife strip, not in a drawer.

Heatproof spatula
Better than a wooden spoon, a heatproof spatula (silicone is great) can scrape the sides and bottom of the saucepan to ensure nothing ends up burning. It can also be used for gently folding batter.

Digital scales
I used to teach French baking to American tourists in Paris and I was constantly trying to convince them that weighing ingredients is an absolute must when it comes to baking. So invest in one of these! It also comes in handy when measuring liquids (1 ml = 1 g), meaning no liquid measuring cup is needed and you can be accurate to the decimal point.

Oven thermometer

I use ovens in many different kitchens, and no matter what the thermometer says on the appliance, it is more often than not incorrect. Having an additional oven thermometer is a good way to make sure the temperature is correct for baking.

Whisk

When you're buying a whisk, look for one with sturdy metal "spokes." Flimsy ones mean it will take longer to whip egg whites and cream.

Fine-mesh sieve

Doubles for sifting lumps out of confectioners' sugar or draining liquids.

Springform cake pan

Probably the most popular size when it comes to baking is 8-in diameter. A springform with its easy release lever will limit the risk of cakes sticking to the sides.

Cutting board (wood or plastic)

If you want to take good care of your knives, make sure never to chop on a glass or marble surface. Don't drag the knife blade across the board to scrape ingredients into a pot, instead turn the blade upside down to scrape. Using the blade to scrape the board is the quickest way of blunting the blade.

Not a must but some additional favorites:

Japanese mandoline

Comes in handy for making equally thin sliced potatoes for your gratin. The grater blade for julienne vegetables makes the crunchiest slaw (rather than a soggy one). Just make sure to be careful and use the hand guard!

Microplane grater

Perfect for zesting citrus fruit as it takes only the fine layer of zest rather than the pith, and equally useful for finely grating hard cheeses.

Piping bag with a set of piping tips

If you're a budding baker, then a good piping bag (go for the silicone-coated ones, which can be easily cleaned, rather than the old-fashioned cloth ones) and a set of piping tips (star shaped and round) are a must.

Containers

Whenever I use up a jar of jam or honey it gets washed out and used to store dry ingredients—it's much better than having open packages lying around. In addition to jam jars, I also have a selection of good-quality airtight containers; they're perfect for storing leftovers in the refrigerator or freezer.

Flat and angled metal spatulas

I have mini (5-in) spatulas, both angled and straight, as well as large ones. They make easy work of icing cakes and the larger ones are handy for moving cakes around. They're also great for lifting up ingredients to see whether the item is cooked underneath.

oven thermometer

whisk

sieve

springform
cake pan

chopping
board

piping bag
and tips

Japanese mandolin

microplane grater

Chile sauce

Eggs

Butter

Cheese

Tinned tomatoes

Puy or Beluga lentils

fresh herbs

Flaky sea salt

Wine vinegar

Ingredients & Cook's Notes

This is a little glimpse into my refrigerator and kitchen cupboards. You'll always find these ingredients hanging about, even if I haven't been grocery shopping recently.

Eggs

I love eggs whether they're fried, poached, or soft boiled, hence I'll spend a little more for eggs with a rich yolk. You can see the difference when you make a pastry cream (such as for the Rhubarb and Custard Millefeuille on page 188), as it will have a richer yellow hue, making it more appetizing. For me, a fried egg served sunny-side up will immediately brighten even the dullest gray winter's day.

The recipes in this book were made using large free-range (and organic) eggs. I tend to keep them at room temperature in my kitchen as I get through them quickly and it makes them less likely to crack when cooking them for a soft-boiled egg. For baking also, it is handy to have all your ingredients at room temperature when you start.

Butter

My mantra "butter makes everything better" stems from my Austrian grandma's love of the golden stuff. I don't need to say much about how adding a knob of butter to a dish will give it a smooth taste. You can even try your hand at making your own on page 239.

Cheese

To say I love cheese is an understatement. I have a serious problem. There's always a piece of cheese (preferably the pungent kind) in my refrigerator. Paired with a few cornichons or pickled onions and some crackers, it's the lazy, but delicious, dinner I turn to when I've been cooking all day.

Crème fraîche (or thick Greek yogurt for the lighter days)

A versatile ingredient; a simple blob of the creamy stuff with some fresh berries and a drizzle of melted chocolate, and dessert is sorted. Also perfect for salad dressings, adding to soups, or making sauces.

Salt

For seasoning I always use a flaky sea salt such as Maldon.

Meat

Always buy the best-quality meat you can afford. I prefer not to eat it if I am unsure of how it was raised, so I try hard to source mine from trustworthy suppliers. I am also a big fan of slow-cooking cuts and offal, which are tastier in my opinion and far more affordable that chicken breasts or fillets of beef.

Fish

I am fortunate to have access to an excellent local fishmonger that only sells fish caught in a sustainable manner. Don't be afraid to ask your fishmonger where the fish comes from.

Fresh herbs

Even living in the city I still have a window box or two with plenty of herbs and the odd radish growing in it. It's much cheaper and significantly more rewarding than buying them. Before the cold winter hits your harvest, pop your herbs in the freezer.

Wine vinegar

I prefer to dress my salads with red or white wine vinegar, rather than balsamic, which can be overbearingly sweet and sticky. Wine vinegar has a cleaner taste. I also use it in sauces to add a of bit acidity when needed, such as in my Summer Spaghetti Bolognese Sauce on page 135 or my Chilled Cucumber Soup on page 53.

Chile sauce

I have at least three types of chile sauce in my refrigerator: a sweet one (perfect for dipping spring rolls, like my own chile sauce on page 251), a fiery one (I love spicy food and will often use chile sauce like a kid would liberally use tomato ketchup), and Tabasco—perfect for seasoning a Bloody Mary.

Canned tomatoes

Sweeter and more flavorful than their plum cousins. I've used them in quite a few recipes, such as my cream of tomato soup on page 18 or the seafood chili on page 94.

Lentils—Puy or beluga

I always feel a little virtuous when I eat lentils, unlike when I eat pasta or potatoes. You might call me a lentil snob, as I prefer the slightly more expensive type, but both Puy and beluga hold their shape better than regular brown lentils and have a delicious nutty flavor.

Cook's Notes

Space to add your own scribbles and doodles

Index

Page references in **bold** indicate photographs

v indicates a vegetarian recipe

gf indicates a gluten-free recipe

Acknowledgments

Thank you!

Like the old saying "behind every successful man is a strong woman" goes, a similar thing could be said about a successful food writer. Behind the scenes there is a brilliant team of people who support my writing and ensure the book is the best it can be. Without these people there would be no book. So a BIG thank-you to:

my publisher: Penguin and the fantastic team at Michael Joseph

my editors: Lindsey Evans and Tamsin English

my art director: John Hamilton

my photographer: David Loftus

my food stylist: Frankie Unsworth

my prop stylists: Lydia Brun and Olivia Wardle

my literary agent: Lizzy Kremer, Harriet Moore, and the team at David Higham

my assistants and recipe tester: Libby Davis, Helen Vass, Charlie Phillips, and Bren Parkins-Knight

And last but not least, my friends, family, and Robert Wiktorin.

And the following brands
for the lovely clothes:

Petit Bateau

Mrs Pomeranz

And the following shops and brands for
lending us some beautiful props:

Rockett St George

The Deli Downstairs

Fired Earth
(special thanks to Elizabeth of Mar)
Most of the Fired Earth tiles used for
the purpose of this shoot are wall tiles
and not suitable for surfaces. For more
info on their tiles, please visit
www.firedearth.com

Present and Correct
(special thanks to Neal)

Le Creuset

The Salvation Army

Anthropologie

Leila's general store

Julia Smith ceramics